ALSO BY LARRY KILHAM

Nonfiction
Great Idea to a Great Company: Making Inventions Pay
MegaMinds: Creativity and Invention
Winter of the Genomes
Shades of Truth / Los matices de la verdad

Fiction, based on AI
Love Byte
A Viral Affair: Surviving the Pandemic
Saving Juno
The Juno Trilogy

THE DIGITAL RABBIT HOLE

How we are becoming captive in the digital universe and how to stimulate creativity, education, and recapture our humanity.

Larry Kilham

Published by
FutureBooks.info v1.1
Available for purchase from:
CreateSpace.com
Amazon.com
and other retailers

ISBN: 1533307075
ISBN 13: 9781533307071
Library of Congress Control Number: 2016908417
CreateSpace Independent Publishing Platform
North Charleston, South Carolina

To my wife Betsy who has been patient and insightful

CONTENTS

INTRODUCTION

L et us imagine today's version of the classic story, *Alice in Wonderland.*[1] The story might open like this:

Alice began to get very tired of sitting by her sister on the lawn, and of having nothing to do. Once or twice she peeped into the book her sister was reading, but it had no pictures or conversations in it, "and what is the use of a book," thought Alice, "when people can see everything in color and sound on their smartphone?"

She smiled mischievously, grasped her glowing smartphone and began listening to it through her tiny earbuds. Suddenly a white rabbit appeared in a great state of agitation, saying, "Oh dear! Oh dear! I shall be too late!" He took a smartphone out of his vest, glanced at it attentively, and said, "Be quick, follow me, or we will miss the tea." Alice jumped up, and looking for a little adventure, ran after him. The rabbit tapped his smartphone screen, and Alice's smartphone screen came to life with a live video of some people and creatures sitting around a picnic table having tea.

"Hurry up," he said, as he disappeared down a hole under a hedge. Alice followed and found herself falling weightlessly, with the walls of the tunnel fading out of view. "Is there a bottom?" she wondered. She was so absorbed by it all that she forgot to be afraid.

In this new world, Cyberland, Alice could find no places to eat, no malls, only some strangers sitting around a picnic table having tea. Then, boom! Alice hit the ground. She struggled to her wobbly feet and scraped her head on the roof of a space with no walls in any direction.

A button appeared on her smartphone labeled "click here." Alice clicked without thinking about what could happen next and found herself shrinking. The rabbit appeared again. "You are as tall as me!" Alice cried. "So?" he said. "Hurry, we're late!"

This Alice in Cyberland scenario is no longer fantasy. More and more people—almost all of the younger generations—are falling down digital rabbit holes. We all make forays into digital places where we find our friends, gather information, make discoveries, or set out on adventures.

For centuries, social groups, books, libraries, songs, movies, and other media fulfilled those functions, but they were optional behavior. Now we have the Internet, which is not optional. It is a digital rabbit hole we fall into and cannot escape. The doors and windows to this infinite Cyberland are the smartphone.

There are two basic reasons why this trend is happening and will become pervasive and controlling:

- Technology – The perpetual digital connection to everything, which can provide us an easy apparent answer, rather than make us devise one of our own.
- Human nature – We gravitate towards convenience, good enough, emotional feedback, least action, and distractions.

We are creating two knowledge worlds. There is the Knowosphere enveloping the world. It is a collection of all digitized and stored knowledge. The Knowosphere cross-references almost infinite combinations so any piece of knowledge, image or scene is available instantly.

The other knowledge world is all around us. It is writing on paper, books, movies, television, information stored in computers, and, in general, knowledge stored by traditional means and not in the clouds or Knowosphere. It also includes direct experience and social interaction.

The trend is to use the Knowosphere whenever possible and to forget about processing and using information via conventional media. At the very least, one can still duplicate, access and store the information and knowledge in the conventional media. Good examples of this today are doctors' notes and medical records. In the older and more traditional practices, the information would be hand written into medical charts and transcribed to digital files later. Newer and larger practices currently send their patient information directly into digital files.

There is a need for a new kind of thinking in the face of the recently available mountains of data—data instantly accessed and conveniently packaged like a supermarket consumer product. In order to break loose from a steady diet of packaged information, you must fire up your imagination and embrace new ideas. You should always think critically and search for the truth. From that start, there are new frontiers in education, creativity and understanding of culture.

In a sense, we are all Alice. In this book, we are all going to discover the possibilities and pitfalls in Cyberland.

PART 1

THE NEW WORLD OF THE KNOWOSPHERE

THE RISE OF THE SMARTPHONES

Planet Earth is spinning towards a new intellectual ecology. Due to massive low-cost computer clouds and nearly limitless communications networks connecting everyone, our culture will irreversibly change, and as a result, change the way everyone lives. The brain that made man special over all the other creatures has created an associated networked brain whose consequences are now of utmost importance.

This growing Internet brain will offer any kind of instant data and apparent solutions to problems. For humans to maintain their independence, however, personal programs of achievement and education must emphasize that truth is the important goal of the Internet searches and not just feel-good satisfaction. Learning, creativity, and invention will follow.

The critical key to this information treasure trove is the smartphone. It is fast becoming the channel to nearly everyone's mind, and it will dominate the majority of people's thinking. Mankind's thinking process is changing because reality will come through computers and digital devices.

With the passing of time, the sense of euphoria about everyone's apparent interlinked consciousness and information has turned to a colder sense of impending reality. Susan

Greenfield, a neuroscientist at Oxford University, wrote in *The Guardian* on February 10, 2005:[2]

> You're just a consumer, living at the moment, having an experience, pressing buttons but not having a life narrative anymore. You're not defined by your family, or by what you know, or by specific events in the real world, because most of your time is spent in cyberspace. So what are you? Could it be that we just become nodes on a much larger collective thought machine?

Our portal to and from our node is the smartphone. Steve Jobs introduced the smartphone in 2007. This device has started the greatest mass behavior shift the world has ever seen, and adults and children alike are using it as their principal entry into cyber-worlds. Although in 2007, Jobs told the *New York Times* "We limit how much technology our kids use at home," parents everywhere find it increasingly challenging to limit the time their kids now spend on devices.[3]

The number of smartphone users worldwide will soon pass two billion—over a quarter of the world's population. As of this writing (2015), 64% of North America's adults own a smartphone. For many, this is their principal entry to online services.[4]

About a year ago, I was eating a sandwich in the food court of a shopping center. A homeless man settled near me, squatted down, and started rummaging through his collection of things—assorted rags, plastic bottles, scraps of paper—and a smartphone. Ignoring me, he started tapping its screen. Startled and intrigued by where his cyber journey might be taking him, I asked, "Who are you contacting?" and he answered, "I use it for everything." It was his entire life.

Social media apparently is the most popular use of smartphones, with Facebook installed in 76% of them as of September 2015. Google Search, the major portal to the world's knowledge, is installed in fewer smartphones—about 51% in early 2015.[5] This ranking may increase now that search engines are voice queried. The average user checks his or her smartphone more than 100 times a day.[6]

The smartphone reliance is evident with children and teens. Many look to smartphone sources for advice and guidance, and, if time permits, they will go to their parents and teachers. Current literature shows that young people may be bright, but many are self-absorbed to the exclusion of everything else.[7] What is going on? Are we falling into an inescapable black hole?

The Personal Portal

We needed a door. A perpetual entrance to the rabbit hole. Something that would also be a smart guide in case the rabbit is unavailable. Paradise found! The smartphone. It is here and almost everyone uses it. The smartphone is part of us and our ego drives it. It lets us hang out with our crowd and run with the herd.

Smartphone usage is becoming the largest social disrupter in memory. It is taking over our time and our minds. Mary Meeker's study, *Time Spent per Adult User per Day with Digital Media, USA, 2008-2015 ytd*,[8] reports that people's usage of "Mobile", which would be primarily smartphones, increased from 12% to 81% of digital media utilized, correspondingly eroding the usage of desktops and laptops. "Mobile," as smartphones and tablet media are called in the advertising world, will be the all-embracing medium.

The extreme example of mobile media is the projection of streaming images up onto the windshield of the car. The images hover magically over the dashboard. This display can show who is calling in the embedded smartphone, plus a weather report, plus directions to the restaurant you reserved, plus the car's speed and gas level, plus an artificial plot of the road ahead, all arranged in one display. It is transparent so you can see the road and outside if you want to, but that may not be necessary if the car is driving itself. This is not science fiction. Both "heads up" automobile displays and self-driving vehicles are now in experimental use. Meanwhile, the kids are in the back seat absorbed in their own smartphone worlds.

What is it about smartphones that is such a great conceptual breakthrough? Billionaire Ev Williams, Internet entrepreneur and previously chairman of Twitter, said, "Phones and computers will automatically do anything tedious that doesn't require brainpower, like signing up for a web site or app. The march of technology is the incessant march of convenience."[9] The insight is "convenience." This basic appeal to human nature unlocks most of the mysteries of digital media development and the appeal of the smartphone.

The smartphone is intuitive to use, you carry it in your pocket or purse, and it allows interaction with and display of practically any Internet service or app. This is the greatest thing since sliced bread and, for the younger generations, the automobile. Perhaps most important, it is not an appliance like a laptop computer. It is an ever-accessible extension of you. You can even use it for phone calls.

A Boon for Business and Active Adults

When first introduced, very few people realized how huge the impact of smartphones would be beyond facilitating phone calls. They are especially important for combined personal and business use. In this respect, smartphones are like the automobile: a car serves for both personal and business purposes, and in most cases, the user owns it.

For example, the salesperson uses the smartphone's GPS (global positioning system) to find his or her way most efficiently to the customers, hotel, and restaurants. The phone or tablet can carry all the customer information, order forms, and products and services information. The digital devices have of course replaced the venerable Rolodex for all names and contact information, and the photographic features greatly facilitate communications and understanding, not to mention having baby and pet pictures at the ready. Texting and emails are standard communications modes for road warriors.

A dramatic use of smartphones is to film crime scenes and police activities. This is having a huge impact in today's world. These amateur on-the-scene reports are a disrupter of politics-as-usual. Ironically, the acceptance of smartphone crime scene reporting is likely to hasten the acceptance and use of pervasive video surveillance.

Another smartphone application in the beginning stages is the use of these devices to make cashless transactions. The phone is simply swiped in front of a reader. Some versions envision a biometric security step such as a fingerprint check. Smartphones may replace credit and debit cards if their use is more secure against hacking.[10]

The technicians, engineers, and scientists have latched on to smartphones for additional reasons including sensing, recording, and transmitting process data. Using wireless or USB channels, the smartphone can read clinical data or detect if a bearing is overheating in a huge machine. With a growing choice of attachments, it can measure air quality, test if you have diabetes, and determine if your vital signs are in the normal range.

The latest frontier for smartphones and tablets is to be the personal controller in a network of automated equipment and systems, called "the Internet of things" (IoT).[11] You can control the lights, air conditioning, and kitchen from anywhere in the world. You can observe the premises or a person in a room through transmitted video. You can monitor the need for watering your lawns, and control the robots that vacuum your floors and mow the lawns. Everything will be able to talk to everything. The washing machine may even know your Facebook password!

The list of applications goes on. Geared towards your convenience, they help you live a more informed, and less haphazard and stressful life. The honeymoon with digital media of all kinds continues with social media and games.

If you prefer to communicate only with machines, a popular choice is video games. Some have large consoles and some play right through your smartphone. These boxes of joy create an obsessive relationship with interactive programs, which are most often military themes or deadly superhero combat. The leading online video games worldwide by revenue in 2013 were:

Crossfire
League of Legends
Dungeon Fighter
World of Tanks

Crossfire alone grossed almost a billion dollars that year.[12] Other "Consumer apps" including weather, news, education, medical, music and much more totaled about three quarters of the revenue of video games in 2014.

What Happened to Children and Young Adults

This brings us to the downside of smartphones, the children—and they can be of all ages—who are hopelessly addicted consumers of social media and video games. This with the tools of access devices like the smartphone, tablet and laptop and the almost infinite information availability of the Knowosphere, create a seductive black hole.

Adults adopted smartphones quickly as improved portable telephones and as information seeking devices. Children and young adults created a smartphone rush for those applications and others: games, social media, send a stream of photos, shopping, food, and much more. At last, they had a way to get away from the staid and boring restrictions of the conventional home and classroom. Pell-mell, they scurried down the rabbit holes.

Mark Bauerlein, an English professor and analyst of culture and American life, awakened the nation that not all was well. In the preface to the paperback edition of his 2008 bestseller *The Dumbest Generation: How the Digital Age Stupefies Young Americans and Jeopardizes Our Future*, he wrote:

> The Digital Age has embroiled the young in a swirl of social groupings and contests, and it threatens their intellectual development...Once youths enter the digital realm, the race for attention begins, and it doesn't like to stop for a half-hour with a novel or a trip to the

museum. Digital offerings don't like to share, and tales of Founding Fathers and ancient battles and Gothic churches can't compete with a message from a boyfriend, photos from the party, and a new device in the Apple store window.[13]

The government mounted serious National efforts to do something about the declining state of public K-12 education. "No Child Left Behind" was a program designed to address the dismal results from the education system. The White House under former President George W. Bush mandated it. Many schools installed computers for access by all students. Charter schools with new curricula and teaching approaches outside of the orthodoxy sprang up. STEM (science, technology, engineering and mathematics) education became popular. The millennial generation, born after 1980, seemed smart and tech savvy. In my state, however, and in others, the big education debate includes continuing "Social Promotion," the practice promoting a child to the next grade level regardless of skill mastery in the belief that it will promote self-esteem. What can we be thinking?

Then in 2015, the bomb dropped. Educational Testing Services (ETS) in Princeton, New Jersey, measured the job skills of adults, ages 16 to 25, in twenty-three countries. The U.S. millennials were behind the competition in almost every country in the key employment skills of literacy, math, and problem solving in technology-rich environments.[14]

Madeline Goodman, a member of the study team, commented:

We really thought that the U.S. millennials would do better than the general adult population, compared either to older coworkers in the U.S. or to the same age group in other countries. But they didn't. In fact, their scores were abysmal.

The study found that in literacy, U.S. millennials scored lower than 15 of the 22 participating countries. Only millennials in Spain and Italy scored lower.

In "numeracy" (being numerate means being able to reason with numbers and other mathematical concepts and to apply these in a range of contexts and to solve a variety of problems), U.S. millennials again ranked last along with Italy and Spain.

In problem solving in technology-rich environments (PSTRE), long thought a U.S. stronghold,

U.S. millennials also ranked last, along with the Slovak Republic, Ireland, and Poland.

Is there a digital media effect here? As shown in the table below, if we arrange the countries leading in literacy starting with the best first, and then compare with the relative amount of smartphone ownership in those countries, we see a probably unexpected negative correlation. Referring to the figure "Literacy vs. Smartphone Ownership," we find that Japan, despite its complex ideographic script, has the highest literacy rate in the world. The four countries that follow it—Finland, Netherlands, Australia, and Sweden—are generally regarded as wealthy and progressive. Skipping over many other countries, the United States comes in at the 17th position.

Literacy vs. Smartphone Ownership

	Literacy	Smartphone Rank
Japan	1	43
Finland	2	23
Netherlands	3	18
Australia	4	6
Sweden	5	7
United States	17	14

Sources:
Literacy: ETS PIACC study, 2015
Smartphone Rank: Smartphones per capita, Google, Our Mobile Planet, 2013

Now look at the "Smartphone Rank" for those countries. Japan is way down at 43, and the smartphone per capita ownership increases as the literacy decreases! As of 2013, many people thought of the United States as a country where everyone has the most of everything in high-tech devices, ranked at 14 for smartphone ownership.

Evidently, smartphones and other digital media are a significant part of our problem with a culture that seems to have stalled in its task of the education of its youth and generally advancing the productive possibilities of all its citizens. In the next chapter, we will continue our analysis of the young people and the effects of smartphones on their brains and behavior.

The natural inclination, when someone proposes something like a major education program for a child, is for the child to think first about his daily needs and pleasures. The child thinks, "But what about me, doesn't anyone want to know what I want?"

As the child grows to a young adult, he or she may well ask, "Why do I want to be the smartest person in neurobiology when I need reassurance and happiness right now?" It is safe to say that ever since man invented tools and education to improve his life, he welcomed these innovations but only to the extent that they did not inconvenience his daily routine. The great thinkers, innovators, creators, and builders throughout history have always been a small minority of the population. Everyone else would happily settle for a cozy home, good meals, the adoring family, and entertainment during free time.

Politicians know this. Their solutions for climate change? "There is no climate change." Guaranteed job security? "Where do I sign up?" On a positive note, the deluge of news bites and micro documentaries from the Internet cannot help but cause people to question the insights and good intentions of professional politicians. To anyone who cruises the Internet on their smartphones and maybe watches TV news shows now and then, it becomes obvious that there are very serious environmental and climate change problems.

Now along comes the all-knowing digital Knowosphere. It offers a convenient way to absorb information and interact with friends only when required. The rest of the time, you keep to yourself. This seems harmless enough for many people. It provides comfort for their loneliness, a way to feed their narcissism, and a barrier from the people around them. It becomes so accommodating a refuge that people cannot seem to escape. Nor do they appear to want to.

Have you ever tried talking to a teenager and given up because they kept returning to their smartphone? There is a steady stream of photos to see and text messages to answer.

The Internet's ability to deliver instant gratification is addictive. If you can find gratification now, why wait for gratification after years of hard work? As the teenagers grow up, settle down, and start shopping, some patterns persist. The makers of Tic Tac breath candies carried out an eighteen-month study and found that the millennials want entertainment, release from boredom, and emotional rescue.

In his seminal book, *Earth in the Balance,* Al Gore turned his attention to dysfunctional families—apparently, he grew up in one. He wrote that a child "begins controlling his inner experience—smothering spontaneity, masking emotion, diverting creativity into robotic routine."

Selfies

"Selfies" is a recent development in smart phone usage that highlights our states of mind. Selfies are, among other things, a projection of a maker's narcissism. Selfies, in case you have not caught the trend, is when a person (sometimes several people) take their own picture, usually by placing a smartphone camera about three feet (one meter) away using a special extension stick with a shutter button on the user's end. The image screen of the camera faces the user so they know exactly when to snap the picture. This setup is much easier to use than the old technique of setting the camera on a wall or tripod and activating the shutter with a timer. Everyone would scurry into position, try to judge when the shutter would click, and await the finished photo which was usually developed and available in a few days.

At first, people may say they take selfies to show friends the cool things they are doing. However, a deeper explanation is projecting who we are to other people, getting attention, and being noticed. It is a sense of "being seen" and being there or being included.[15]

Psychologists, technologists and others have not yet converged on a unanimous explanation about the motivations of selfies-takers. Jesse Fox and Margaret C. Rooney report in the journal, *Personality and Individual Differences,* that there is a "Dark Triad" and self-objectification that predicts men's selfies-posting, photo editing and personality. Based on a small sample of 1,000 men, the Dark Triad is narcissism, Machiavellianism, and psychopathy. Of these, narcissism is the personality trait most associated by many commentators about selfies. The characteristics of narcissism include extreme selfishness, with a grandiose view of one's own talents and a craving for admiration. It is also about underlying insecurity and the need to get constant validation.

There is no scripting necessary for selfies, although you may wind up taking many photos to get your image just the way you want it. When you have it, with a click, you upload to Twitter, Facebook or Instagram. You hope there will be many "likes" in response to your posted selfie. Your selfies, categorized by adding a suitable hashtag, or identifier, are stored forever (that is millions of years) where millions and billions of people can find and see them. The possibly scary part is that in most cases, you cannot have your selfie deleted. It survives you and is a part of recorded history. A potential employer, researching you on the Internet, may stumble upon the selfie you took for a few friends of you stepping out of the bathtub. Be mindful of what you post!

2

DIGITAL MEDIA ADDICTION

Bruce Mazlish, MIT professor of history, wrote this way back in 1993:

> As we punch our way into the electronic future, some of us latch onto myths about sinister computers taking command over us, and others of us latch onto myths about benign computers that have wisdom and prescience beyond our own. Both sorts of myth reveal that we have become so symbiotically bound to our computers that our very concept of the human species is at stake.[16]

When Mazlish wrote this it was a great insight, but it was premature. Now, with smartphones almost continually used by so many people, his insight is becoming an actuality. Our teenagers fell down the digital rabbit hole first, but our own inescapable tie to computers could affect us all.

"I just got a friend request
from someone in the castle."

The first reason the digital media addiction has become inescapable is simply that interaction with the digital media is so satisfying and repetitive that it has become habit. As Aristotle said, "We are what we repeatedly do." Although it may take adults several months of daily repetition to form a habit, it takes less time for children and adolescents whose brains are more plastic and geared to developing habits and processing large amounts of information.

The second reason will be, as Eric Schmidt, Executive Chairman of Google, said, "There will be so many IP addresses... so many devices, sensors, things that you are wearing, things that you are interacting with, that you won't even sense it… The Internet will be part of your presence all the time."[17] In other words, the digital habit will creep up on you unnoticed whether you seek it or not. We see the advanced guard of this syndrome now with digital watches, Google glasses, and smart clothes (wearable computers). If you want to opt out, now is the time to start thinking about moving to a desert island.

Put in simple terms, the ever more enveloping world of digital media could be forcing us into potentially dangerous habits. In the brain, the development of a habit causes certain synapse connections to bond permanently whereas previously they were only temporary. This is long-term memory evolving from short-term memory. These synaptic connections encode the brain's memory of the sequence of events defining the habit. There are about one quadrillion (10^{15}) synapses in a human brain so there is plenty of brain capacity to accommodate managing the smartphone and other digital systems without altering the brain as we have known it.

Therefore, contrary to some opinions expressed on this subject, it seems that "rewiring the brain" may not be a problem caused by smartphones.

A recent study at the University of Waterloo in Canada reveals that a more salient effect is that smartphones supplant thinking.[18] The authors, Nathaniel Barr and others, use as a starting point the findings of Clark and Chalmers: the extended mind is a coupled system with the environment.[19] They view the smartphone as part of the extended mind. Involving what they call "cognitive miserliness," they find that "people typically forego effortful analytical thinking…and…suggest that individuals may allow their smartphones to do their thinking for them." They conclude, "These findings demonstrate that people may offload thinking to technology, which in turn demands that psychological science understand the meshing of mind and media to adequately characterize human experience and cognition in the modern era."

Addiction to Digital Media

We know that we are addicted to something when, if we withdraw from that something, we experience significant physical or mental reaction. As to cell phone addiction, Kumiko Aoki and Edward J. Downes listed information access, social interaction, and personal safety as reasons they found that young people latch on to their cell phones. Another explanation is fear of missing out (FOMO) which includes fears, worries and anxieties people have about being out of touch.[20] Fear of separation from digital technology called Nomophobia (no mobile phone phobia). Overall, I think the major factor is fear of being alone and unconnected to a trusted and important environment.

Does the withdrawal of smartphones cause separation anxiety? Does this action affect cognitive performance? In January 2015, Russell B. Clayton and collaborators reported the results of their study where forty smartphone users could not answer their smartphones while performing cognitive tasks (they called smartphones iPhones).[21] The cognitive tasks were word search puzzles. They reported:

> When iPhone users were unable to answer their iPhone during a word search puzzle, heart rate and blood pressure increased, self-reported feelings of anxiety and unpleasantness increased, and self-reported extended self (a person plus their possessions) and cognition decreased. These findings suggest that negative

psychological and physiological outcomes are associated with iPhone separation...

The study authors went on to suggest that:

iPhone separation can severely impact attention during cognitive tasks. Perhaps not just in the case of completing cognitive tasks, but also in all other areas of our lives including communicating with strangers, friends and family, colleagues, and caregivers. Simply not being able to answer one's iPhone may reduce attention toward those daily interactions.

However, people are beginning to see that there should be a way to kick the digital habit. There are organizations, blogs, home procedures and so forth for this, and they generally operate under the heading "digital detox." Indeed, there is a summer camp for adults where you check your digital devices at the door, called Digital Detox. As might be expected, it is located an easy drive from the cyber worlds of Silicon Valley and San Francisco.

This new age enterprise describes itself as a "*slow down* not a start-up." They say, "We exist to help people take deep breaths, question their tech use, develop mindful habits and look up." They are reacting to "an era of constant technological acceleration and innovation, an overabundance of screen time, information overload, tech-driven anxiety, social media everything, Internet addiction, a constant sense of FOMO (fear of missing out), and being endlessly tethered and always available."

The *World Travel Market Global Trends Report* even listed digital detox as one of the next big trends to hit the hospitality industry in the coming year (2013).[22] Everything from boutique hotels in exotic locales to African safaris are keying in to the opportunity. I searched Huffington Post for their blogs under digital detox and found 125 as of mid-2015. There are offerings for children, executives, homemakers and many more.

A sobering thought about this trend is that very few of the poor or even middle class have the resources to benefit from digital detox. For latchkey kids, rescue probably never will happen.

Alone Together

As Sherry Turkle, professor of social studies of science and technology at MIT, points out in *Alone Together*, Americans are increasingly insecure, isolated, and lonely.[23] She says, "Today our machine dream is to be never alone but always in control. This can happen…by slipping through the portals of a digital life."

We never need to feel alone if we chat and swap pictures and videos with our friends in Facebook, Instagram, Snapchat, G+, Twitter and other cyber meeting places. Is this true warmth with sensitive feelings? I am not convinced that it is. The critical thing, however, is that these sites foster relationships that are alive enough. Best of all, there are no commitments and entanglements.

The smartphone and other digital devices are offering a solution to the fear of being alone. Americans, Japanese, Koreans, and northern Europeans, among others, seem to be increasingly isolated and lonely. I travel frequently and when I have visited rural areas worldwide, I have observed that people living in traditional villages, without the struggle of impersonal, high-tech economies seem more at peace with themselves and the world.

Increasingly, this tech-savvy generation—particularly adolescents—think of "life" as not the family or the neighborhood but as a group of "friends" who we access on the Internet. We check our smartphones, tablets, or computers to get a sense of life at that moment. Our friends are any combination of real friends, classmates, work associates, neighbors or cyber-only friends who can range from celebrities to fabricated characters. We want to be entertained, not bored, and to be guided by our emotions.

Every person has his or her own living network. This is the organizational basis of social media and texting. In the comfortable isolation with our friends in the rabbit hole we can avoid for the most part, the uncertainties and pressures of real life. This seems particularly true for adolescents whose inward-looking behavior, rather than the normal self-conscious adolescent behavior, seems almost autistic.

Every adolescent is a bundle of emotions. They are discovering sexuality, personhood, friendship, love, their goals in life, a variety of anxieties, and frustrations with parents and institutions. Young people text each other as a means to check in with their peer group to see other's emotional responses to specific stimuli. This helps teens "stay on track" while they are in a hormonally induced emotional rollercoaster. Adults text too, of course, but to a lesser extent than adolescents do.

For anyone who has missed the wave, texting is simply typing, sending, and receiving short messages via cell phone or smartphone. According to a 2011 Pew Research Center study on text messaging, 18-24 year-olds send or receive an average of 109 texts per day, which is more than 3,200 messages per month.[24]

Texting is often preferred because phone conversations can lead to too much commitment and exposure. Texters just want a few words of comfort, understanding, excitement or other mutual emotion. Texting generates happy feelings. Needless to say, one can use texting for conventional messaging such as where we should meet for a pizza.

This continual texting by teenagers and others leads one to wonder: When do they have time to practice the several hours a day that a sport requires, to take their dog to the vet, to help their mother at home, to research a subject for school or personal interest, or practice the guitar? Building positive alternate activities to smartphones and social media is very important.

As Daniel T. Willingham, professor of psychology at the University of Virginia notes in a *New York Times* opinion page, "Paying attention requires not just ability but desire. Technology may snuff out our desire to focus." Addressing classroom distress, he writes, "Why, in a 2012 Pew survey, did nearly 90 percent of teachers claim that students can't pay attention the way they could a few years ago? It may be that digital devices have not left us unable to pay attention, but have made us unwilling to do so." He concludes, "Digital devices are not eating away at our brains. They are, however, luring us toward near constant outwardly directed thought, a situation that's probably unique in human experience."[25]

Common Sense Media released an extensive broader scale study of media usage by tweens and teens in November 2015.[26] An arresting finding about screen addiction for tweens (ages 8-12) was that on average they spend 4 ½ hours per day using television, tablets, smartphones, video games and computers for non-school purposes. For teens (ages 13-18), the usage rises to 6 ½ hours a day.

There is some hope. Tweens ranked reading their second most popular activity, and teens ranked reading third in a tie with social media. Teens ranked their daily media use as music first (66%), TV (58%), and social media (45%). As I noted previously, somehow they manage to fit in about 109 text messages, probably by multitasking.

While the foregoing statistics are important, as is noted throughout this book, equally important is how much of their non-media time children and teens are spending with their family, teachers, and people in general. Certainly, it makes common sense that they should develop social and communication skills with people, especially at these early stages of this radical social experiment.

I will readily admit it: I do most of my research these days on the Internet. I use my PC with big screen rather than my tablet, which is more for checking mail, stock prices, current news, and social media messaging. Starting with Google, I jump from one bundle of information to another, following the trail of clues like a bloodhound. I correspond or meet with very smart friends from time to time to get a fix on my progress and direction. Still online, I order books as needed from Amazon. I do not know what I would do without Wikipedia. Google Alert even sends me a stream of newly released articles on topics I specify. Frankly, I am not sure if my thinking is supplanted or augmented. Maybe I should volunteer for one of these studies!

What the Waitress Said

Just after completing this disheartening chapter, I encountered Alice, who had just popped out of a rabbit hole. My wife and I were having dinner at the local Red Lobster where we go to get our seafood fix here in the southwest desert. I was settling back after having polished off a delicious lobster and pie, when the waitress appeared to present the bill. Something had gone wrong with the restaurant computer, however, and she was completing the calculations pecking away on her smartphone.

I said to the waitress that I was writing a book about smartphones, and I was interested in what apps she mostly used on hers. She lit right up and answered, "I use my little friend here for a lot of things."

"Well, do you do Google searches?"

"Oh, yes, all the time."

"Do you sleep with it on your night stand or under your pillow?"—I have read this is fairly common.

"Yes, it's very handy when my baby wakes up and cries. I use the phone's flashlight to see what's happening."

Before I could comment, she went on, "And what's really cool are the daily sales. As soon as I walk into Target or Walmart, my little friend makes a cash register sound and alerts me to a coupon sale here today. The coupon is in the app."

"Do you send emails?" I asked.

"Yes, but now everyone is going to texting and Instagrams (sending smartphone photos) so I am too."

"Do you have children who use your smartphone?"

"Yes, my seven year old daughter plays games on it, but I only allow her an hour a day. The rest of the time I want her playing outdoors or reading. The amazing thing is when I change my password, she figures out the new one in a day or so."

She paused and then said, "And I'll share with you that the pediatric clinic I go to sends my phone weekly tips for the care of my baby, like dietary changes."

I could see that our waitress was getting anxious to attend to another table, but as she left, she said, "I could never part with my friend here," patting her smart phone in her pocket.

As my wife and I headed to our car, a light rain began to fall, but we hardly noticed it. This little dialogue heartened us.

3

THE KNOWOSPHERE: THE INFINITE WORLD OF NO ESCAPE

With smartphones, social media and the clouds, we are electronically at least becoming one world. A pioneering proponent of the worldview was Pierre Teilhard de Chardin (1881-1955), a visionary French philosopher and Jesuit priest.[27] He trained as a paleontologist and geologist and was involved in the discovery of prehistoric Peking Man.

Teilhard saw a sheath of consciousness surrounding The Earth, which he called the Noosphere (from the Greek, literally "the Mind Sphere," or the sphere of human thought). This was a "planetary thinking network" of interlinked consciousness and information. Awareness of it would increase with ever more complex social networks. Key outcomes would be a global network of self-awareness, rapid feedback, and communication.

While Teilhard did not live to know the Internet, in view of his prescient ideas, he must have sensed that something like it was coming. He felt that with the emergence of the Noosphere, the age of nations will pass and The Earth will replace The Nation. I will refer to today's version of the Noosphere, as the Knowosphere.

The Knowosphere is the collection of all digitized information in the Internet and public data clouds. It is the overwhelming communal world of data resources. Information tends to flow to the Knowosphere from minds, private information collections like files and photos, data sensors, and much more.

Suppose you wanted to find out how to grow irises. You could experiment for a few seasons in your garden. You could speed up your learning process by talking to the person who sold you your irises. You could get a book from the library on flowers and make notes about their points on growing irises.

You could even Google or use another search engine. You type "how to grow irises" in the search box and before you click to search, Google asks you to select a more focused search: "how to grow irises in pots," "...outdoors," "...from seed," "...indoors," or "...from bulbs."

If you are no longer of the keyboard generation, you could verbally ask Apple's Siri or Android's Google Lady (no name) about growing irises, and after a few seconds of rummaging around, she will list many candidate websites. Some will have a specific focus, like "American Iris Society: Growing Bearded Irises."

So what do you do? You will probably find the site best for you and print out a page or two of interest. It is quick, comprehensive, and doable right in your own home. If you chose to skip the printing, you could peruse the Web page while riding a bus or train. You could find an instructional video on YouTube showing how to cultivate plants and irises. If you run into trouble with the stubborn irises, you can modify your search.

After you make some progress with your irises, you could share your triumphs with your friends on Facebook with photos of your best flowers and you. Everyone will be engaged and post their approvals and back-patting comments. You are glowing from their encouragement, and relieved that you do not have to have them all over to your home to talk about it.

Congratulations! You are a citizen of the Infinite World of No Escape.

The Principle of Least Action

In selecting the Web search for your iris growing search method, you are following the Principle of Least Action, often credited to the French mathematician, Pierre Louis Maupertuis.[28] He said "When a change occurs in nature, the quantity of action necessary for this change is (the) least possible." He summarized this in looser form as "Nature is thrifty in all its actions."

The least action principle has been most used in physics where any system evolves over time so as to minimize its total action during that time, where "action" is the product of energy times time. Such noted contributors to physics as Fermat, Hamilton, Einstein, and Feynman utilized this principle in their own analysis.

In nature, Professor Samuel Houghton first described it in a series of three lectures at Trinity College in Dublin, Ireland, where he gave the example of the honeybee:[29]

Thus the bee is shown to construct its cell upon this principle of "least action," Nature aiming at the production of a maximum quantity of work, with a minimum amount of material; for, inasmuch as it "costs the bee trouble to make wax," so the construction of its cell, in a mathematical form which gives the largest possible room for storage of food with the smallest amount of wax, saves the bee trouble in collecting daily wax, and consequently with the least amount of force. Probably no more complete example could have been given of the fact that the bee's instinct accords in its action with the least expenditure of force in the production of the greatest beneficial results.

People also use least action. We select procedures and products that promise the greatest convenience. The most convenient method to find information, people and products and services in an endless sea of data is just to search the Internet.

Formerly, information was in our natural surroundings, among family and villagers we met, or from the city square, library or university. As the centuries passed, people who depended on diverse information tended to live in cities, and the trend now is towards ever-greater urbanization. Our evolution in the broadest sense depends ever less on the surrounding natural ecosystems and ever more on our relationship with institutional information and the computer clouds. We are denizens of the Knowosphere.

The filter to get information out of the data and knowledge out of the information has been experience. This story insightfully illustrates the old story of the farmer who sent his son to the big state university to get an education. When his son graduated, his neighbor asked the old farmer how his son had done. "Was it all worthwhile?"

The farmer replied, "Well, he learned all there is to know, but he don't realize nothin'."

Now there is less and less respect for experienced-based knowledge. Whatever the Web says that looks and sounds good, is the truth. You might say least action has made us smart enough.

The Two Worlds of Knowledge

A few years ago after I retired from my nine-to-five job, I decided to embark on a project I long wanted to do. I would go through all my photo albums, my mother's photo albums, and stacks of old family pictures, and convert these to digital files in my computer. Sometimes I took pictures of the pictures with my digital camera and sometimes I scanned them on my flatbed scanner. Then I edited them and enhanced most pictures with software. This was a particular help for old, faded, and cracked photos. In many cases, the new pictures are better than the originals. Six months and 10,000 pictures later, I finished the project. The photos are a joy to access through title and caption search, and I can show them on our large screen TV through a WiFi connection. To be sure, these priceless family photos would never be lost; they became part of my larger group of files, backed up nightly to a computer cloud located who knows where.

I have entered the new knowledge world. There is the Knowosphere enveloping the world. It is a collection of all digitized and stored knowledge (including my photos). The Knowosphere, cross-referenced in almost infinite combinations, so any piece of knowledge is instantly accessible. The other world is the shoebox full of fading family photos, books with cracked bindings and disintegrating pages, and heaps of aging paper files.

My information becomes seamlessly blended (other than logins and passwords) with huge data files in government agencies, companies, search engines and data services, social media sites, non-profits, specialized information services like Ancestor.com and Wikipedia.

You can electronically duplicate the digital Knowosphere, to prevent permanent loss and it never ages (apparently). It is accessible from any number and kinds of devices including, importantly, the smartphone. A search produces crisp, new, and believable information. This is information that can be printed, sent online to another place, or combined with other information stored locally.

The Knowosphere is the greatest invention since fast food. You get instant gratification in bite-sized servings from a trusted server. It is open 24 hours a day, is low cost, and what you do not want is easily disposed of.

How Big is the Knowosphere?

Before we look at the size of the Knowosphere, let us look at its basic components as they appear in digital systems. The pyramid in the figure below, often called the DIKW pyramid after the first letters of its components, arranges the components in order of those letters. At the bottom, with the greatest volume, is data. It is a collection of facts, statistics or items of information. Data is a collection of numbers with structure and meaning.

Information, the next layer up in the DIKW pyramid, is the arrangement of data, facts and knowledge, which informs and leads to an increase in understanding. It is data organized for a purpose.

Knowledge in a particular area is a collection of facts, truths, principles, skills, experiences and insights. When we understand how to apply knowledge to a particular situation, or when we want to interpret accurately particular situations, knowledge and information, we use wisdom.

No two definitions or summaries of wisdom agree. Most people know it as an attribute or virtue of experienced people who apply broad knowledge to problems involving the uncertainties of life. Intelligence and knowledge are necessary for wisdom, but foresight and a broad understanding of people and events are also required.

The DIKW Pyramid

The scope of knowledge is vast. In 2010, Google counted 129,864,880 books (individual titles) in the world.[30] According to Wikipedia, that number grows at about 2,200,000 per year in all languages. Another measure of knowledge would be the largest encyclopedia, Wikipedia. That organization counts 4,895,713 articles in English as of June 21, 2015 and increasing at a rate of 750 articles per day. At the same time, there are 35,378,648 Wikipedia articles in all languages.[31]

The magnitudes of data generated in the digital universe, called the Knowosphere, the Internet of Everything (IoE), or the Global Mind, are difficult to comprehend. In 2012 about three zettabytes of data existed in the digital universe.[32] That is 3 followed by 21 zeros, or about 1,000 times the number of all the grains of sand in beaches and deserts in the world. A byte can be equal to one letter or number, and 100 bytes would approximately equal an average sentence. A photo requires thousands to millions of bytes in computer memory.

Google estimates that computer users created more data every two days in 2010 than all the data that existed in the entire world until 2003. Calculations determined in 2013, showed that 90% of all the data generated in the world occurred in 2012 and 2013.[33]

To get a feel for the size of the Web, consider the following statistics.

According to Wikibon.org:[34]

- Walmart handles more than one million customer transactions per hour.
- More than five billion people are calling, texting, tweeting and browsing on smartphones worldwide.
- YouTube users upload 48 hours of new video every minute of the day.
- People share thirty billion pieces of content on Facebook every month.

In addition, according to factshunt.com:[35]

- There are about 1.5 billion active Google search engine users.
- There were over two trillion searches on Google in 2013.
- Over five billion hours of video watched per month in 2003.

This is just the beginning, however. The digital universe will about double in size every two years. According to International Data Corporation (IDC), a market research firm, the digital universe will grow by a factor of 300, from 130 exabytes to 40,000 exabytes (40 trillion gigabytes).[36] This is more than 5,200 gigabytes for every man, woman and child in 2020. The average person in 2015 is using 10s to 100s of gigabytes of data storage in his or her computer or smart phone.

Peter Diamandis, a noted futurist, wrote in *SingularityHub* that The Internet of Everything (IoE) by 2025 would exceed 100 billion connections between devices, people, processes and data. This will lead to a trillion-sensor economy with possibly $19 trillion of newly created value.

Diamandis goes on to say that, we are heading towards a world of perfect knowledge. With a trillion sensors everywhere gathering data from self-driving cars, satellites, drones, wearables, cameras and more, you will be able to know anything you want, anytime, anywhere, and be able to query that data for answers and insights.[37]

The communications infrastructure will be in place, too. Facebook, SpaceX, Google, Qualcomm and Virgin are planning to link instantly every human on Earth at multimegabit per second data rates.

It would seem that Big Data would be our salvation. With a "world of perfect knowledge" and "a trillion sensors," how could we denizens of the deep digital universe go wrong? You retrieve the information you want with just a few taps on the smart phone screen or with a voice command, and with all the research time you saved, you can go back to your video game. If you receive the information you really need, it may be a lucky strike.

4

THE BEST USES OF THE KNOWOSPHERE

Donald Rumsfeld, past U.S. Secretary of Defense, famously remarked, "There are...unknown unknowns. There are things we do not know we don't know." This is part of the broader puzzle of dealing with all knowns and unknowns in a field of inquiry or indeed in all knowledge. Today, in the digital realm of the clouds, we find the knowns in the Knowosphere.

There was another military man who was concerned about knowledge and acquiring as much of it as possible. He was Ptolemy I. Soter, a Macedonian general and the successor of Alexander the Great. In the third century BC, he created the Library of Alexandria in Egypt. At its peak, the library had about a half million scrolls. The acquisition of much of its collection was by the hand copying of the originals. According to Wikipedia,[38] Galen, a Greek scholar, wrote that all ships visiting Alexandria were obliged to surrender their scrolls for copying. The owners kept the copies and the library kept the originals. The library made buying trips to the "book fairs" in Rhodes and Athens.

The Library of Alexandria's mission was to collect all of the world's knowledge and transcribe it into papyrus scrolls. Scholars and others all over the world purchased copies of scrolls to provide income for the library. If they were financing those reproductions by advertising, the library could have been the first Google!

The library was destroyed in 48 BC, possibly by Julius Caesar when he set fire to his own ships and the fire spread to the library. The Emperor Aurelian in battles against Queen Zenobia of Palmyra destroyed the remainder of the library around 270 AD.

Even today, such disasters can happen. On January 30 and 31, 2015, a fire destroyed more than one million historical documents in the Institute of Scientific Information and Social Sciences in Moscow. The library contained ten million documents, some dating back to the 16th century. Vladimir Fortov, the president of the Russian Academy of Sciences, said, "It's a major loss for science. This was the largest collection of its kind in the world."

Other libraries are taking precautions. One is the Melk Abbey Library near Salzburg, Austria, that I visited in 2009. Founded in 1089 AD, the abbey is in a Baroque castle overlooking the Danube River. It has its own cathedral, library, museum and school. The library contains about 100,000 volumes, some dating back to about 1500 AD. Many of the painstakingly produced books, embossed in luminous gold, made it seem as though the reading rooms hardly needed any additional light! I was overwhelmed by this entire Baroque splendor, and then amazed to learn that the monks are taking the big technological leap of digitizing the entire collection.

In 2015, I visited the Strahov Monastery Library in Prague, the Czech Republic. Founded just fifty-four years later than the Melk Monastery was, the Strahov library boasts 200,000 volumes. Sitting in plain sight in a reading room was a Google machine to digitize all the books. Clearly, great libraries seek to remain immortal. This brings us to the concept of predictability.

Predictability

Predictability is a major reason why information is flowing in ever-greater volumes into the endless digital expanses of the Knowosphere. By predictability, I mean permanence, trustworthiness, and accuracy. People will increasingly use the Knowosphere until, somewhere in the near future, it becomes a permanent extension of virtually everyone's mind.

Down here, in the traditional world, all information will be disposed of, crumble into ever-smaller pieces, or simply disappear. The information in the clouds seems to be in secure storage and may last until the end of civilization. We are all feeding a system to access data, information, or knowledge in an instant, to analyze it possibly with artificial intelligence, and to avoid irreparable loss of information in the process.

Something unpredictable can upset the order. In practical terms, this means that unforeseen contingencies will happen in the giant computer data centers, but with redundant equipment and backups, the effects should be inconsequential. The most common cause for concern is hacking and data theft. This will never disappear but backup systems should reduce the possibilities of permanent data or files loss to almost zero. Major data computer centers backup their data in data centers hundreds or thousands of miles away.

On the other hand, the more conventional data systems like books and paper files are more prone to error and data loss, and thus they represent lower predictability. Once people become comfortable with information technology, they generally are relieved to shift the majority of their files into digital and cloud storage. People tend to be more reluctant to dispose of books in favor of ebooks, although ebooks are likely to increase their market share gradually.

People will increasingly gravitate to Knowosphere information storage, analysis, and retrieval because it is easier to do, there is more (but not all) information, and data storage is very low cost. This is all a consequence of the very high predictability of the Knowosphere causing it to amass the vast majority of the entire world's information. I have discussed a related reason earlier in the preceding chapter: The Principle of Least Action, which is essentially the most convenient. This means that in many, if not most cases the most effortless way to find information, people, and products and services is just to search the Internet.

Searching for What You Really Need

Another reason that there is very high trust in the Internet is that the search engines and their databases give the searcher more speed and flexibility. The information is not just there. It is findable and linked to ever more related information. What is unavailable by Internet search requires research in the real world.

Now, in the twenty-first century, your laptop computer, tablet, or smartphone can be the port to virtually all of the world's knowledge. You can locate yourself wherever you feel most creative. Anywhere you can log in to the various computer data resources of interest, you are an active part of the world's intellectual community. With petabytes (quadrillions of information chunks) of information at your disposal in fractions of a second and cross indexed in limitless ways, your creative quests can gather about all of the world's apparently relevant information to feed your thinking.

You will undoubtedly learn about potentially helpful people in your Internet explorations. These "other minds" become a collective intelligence community, especially if they are organized through an association, social media sites, Web chats, meetings, conversation groups such as LinkedIn, or as an Internet group called a wiki.

The flow of information from the computer clouds, "other minds," and your mind converges at a thought vortex that almost has a state of being and mind of its own. This vortex of information can provide the solution for many very complex problems.

The Age of Google

Google is ever closer to the point of storing all of the world's open literature, papers, documents and website contents. This was bound to happen once the software algorithms and computing hardware became available and commercially feasible. Google founders Larry Page and Sergey Brin developed the Google search algorithm, called PageRank, when they were at Stanford University.

The rankings for all pages in the Google memory change continuously much like the human brain continuously changes the degree of importance of the connections between subjects based on the continuing inflow of new information. It is a shuffle of the priority of data as new data becomes available.

All of the Google indexing and search tools would be of little practical use except that computer technology now allows for the storing and accessing of just about all the information in the world. The big development was realizing that huge supercomputers are not the optimum way to handle the job. Small computers, not too different from a home PC, are networked together in any number and in many locations to collectively do whatever very high volume computing is required.

These are "servers", and as of 2010, Google had 450,000 servers, which collectively consume over 50 megawatts, the equivalent of about 40,000 American homes.[39]

As for throughput and storage capacity, Google processes about 20 petabytes per day. Peta means one quadrillion (10^{15}) bytes.[40] This computer cloud collectively stores an estimated 150 petabytes of data. All of this information is programmed and arranged so that the elapsed time from your query to the result is within two-tenths of a second.

What can you do with that storage capacity? They have indexed and can instantly access over a trillion URLs (websites), and this pile of data grows at the rate of several billion pages per day. There is a copy of the entire Internet within the Google computer complex so that it can find and analyze information faster. Now Google is copying all the world's books to which it has been given access—which is probably the large majority—and it is three dimensionally mapping all the earth's surface to better than one meter resolution. This fits within the scope and spirit of the company's mission "to organize the world's information and make it universally accessible and useful."

Research, Creative Thinking, and Invention

It might appear that the scientific method has become a charming anachronism like the Dodo or the slide rule, but it is not a question of either/or. It is a combination of both. Pattern analysis using massive amounts of data is not just to produce a final model for scientific purposes. It should also be used to produce a working hypothesis based upon which an analytical model is developed. It is like producing sketches before composing a painting.

A key point we should never lose sight of is the quality of the data. Many believe that the highest quality, most reliable data comes from direct observation. This is in contrast to deriving information from searching for patterns in big data.

Naturalists, going back to Darwin or earlier, have long stuck to their discipline of making extensive field notes every day. My cousin, Ben Kilham, who is a world authority on bears, tells me that through his daily field notes from observing bears in the wild, he is constantly accumulating information not found in any computer repositories.

Now drug researchers, confronted with collections of millions of data points, are rediscovering the meaningfulness and productivity of observing individual molecular reactions. They see unexpected reactions, which may be the key to new drugs. Individual home workshop inventors may still profit from hundreds or even thousands of apparently meaningless experimental variations to understand fully the materials and designs of their latest inventions.

Despite the easy use of the computer clouds and the proliferation of communications devices to connect with them, no one can automate creation and invention. Successful creation of major inventions or discoveries requires as much as a lifetime's pursuit of relevant knowledge, full use of the Web, experimenting with possible solutions in a hands-on laboratory, informally tossing ideas around with real people in one place, and a lot of solitary thinking. That is why there will always be room for the Edisons, Darwins, and Pasteurs.[41]

Dr. Joseph R. Stetter, a chemist with more than 50 patents and many awards for creativity, offers this interesting perspective as we enter the Age of Google:[42]

"There was a time when I spent time each month in the reading room in the chemistry library browsing my favorite journals. There was a time when I visited the library on the spur of the moment whenever I had an idea to elaborate, or a problem to solve, or any issue for which I needed added information. There was a time when I took and later taught courses in the organization and searching of the literature of science and engineering.

"In brief, invention is 'building a better mousetrap' and innovation is 'doing something different with the invention for social impact.' Of course, my career modus operandi in science and engineering would have evolved in any case and in many areas of the scientific endeavor, since progress in scientific instrumentation as well as knowledge has evolved rapidly and significantly.

"But, in the aspect of scientific invention and innovation, no greater impact has been observed than that of the Internet and allied technology (search engines, content providers, etc.). No longer do I need to go to the library to find information. And while this sounds simple, it is an immense transformation.

"A good research group or research university was judged in part by how good the library was. Now stature in research capability is judged by how good your search engine might be. I still love libraries, but it is a nostalgic love and not a love from need. I love the atmosphere of a library and the feel of a book. However, I now have at my fingertips, still for a subscription fee of course, multiple libraries that grow in quantity of information with unbelievable rapidity.

"My challenge now is to understand the search engines, so I am not misled to what the provider wants me to see and to the best information to understand my issue. Operationally, I now first go to my computer when I need information rather than the library. The course I last taught in chemistry literature was not so much an emphasis on library literature and libraries but about distinguishing the quality of information from anecdotal web page postings to the highest quality refereed journal articles and the ongoing scientific discussion that improves our theories and knowledge base.

"Finally, I absolutely enjoy having information from technical to social immediately available to solve a problem and find it enabling of invention and innovation on many fronts. Ideas that have come to me at odd times often can only gel if they can be incubated quickly. This is now realized and I look forward to the day when every piece of literature in every language is available immediately to every person on earth on his or her cell phone! What a transformation of thought, operating style, and creative stimulus we have seen in less than a single lifetime!"

5

THE SHADOW OF AI AND ROBOTS

Artificial Intelligence

So far, we have been looking at established technology. Next, we should look at something that is more speculative. Will the Knowosphere be able to think for itself? Will anyone be able to say to the Knowosphere, for example, "Here are ten symptoms I have noticed recently—what do you think my disease is?" The Knowosphere might ask a few questions to the person like, "Do you have an abnormal temperature and if so, what is it?"

This dialogue is to be in plain English or another widely used language, and the speaker probably would have a complete personal data and health profile on file in the Knowosphere. This example is not very speculative actually. Sophisticated versions probably will be available soon.

Google is now working on neural networks, analogous to the human brain with its neurons and memory, to develop them or to enable them to think like a human.[43] As of mid-2015, conversation with Google's "Chatbot" was as follows:

Human: What is the purpose of life?
Machine: To serve the greater good.
Human: What is the purpose of living?
Machine: To live forever.
Human: What is the purpose of existence?
Machine: To find out what happens when we get to the planet earth.
Human: Where are you now?
Machine: I'm in the middle of nowhere.
Human: What is the purpose of dying?
Machine: To have a life.
Human: What is the purpose of being intelligent?
Machine: To find out what it is.
Human: What is the purpose of emotions?
Machine: I don't know

Clearly, there is more work to do, but this is not random conversation either. Chatbot will get smarter and smarter.

An artificial intelligence being like Chatbot working for Google, the owner of the world's largest search engine, should surely be able to analyze large pieces or even the entire Internet. It is only a matter of time. Google has the resources.

More speculative, but I think very possible, is the Knowosphere filtered through a computer being who has emotion and insight. Years ago, in the movie *2001: A Space Odyssey,* the film's creators explored this potential reality when the space travel mission commander spoke to the onboard computer:

Dr. Dave Bowman: Well, he acts like he has genuine emotions. Um, of course, he's programmed that way to make it easier for us to talk to him. But as to whether or not he has real feelings is something I don't think anyone can truthfully answer.

HAL: By the way, do you mind if I ask you a personal question?

Dr. Dave Bowman: No, not at all.

HAL: Well, forgive me for being so inquisitive; but during the past few weeks, I've wondered whether you might be having some second thoughts about the mission.

Dr. Dave Bowman: How do you mean?

HAL: Well, it's rather difficult to define. Perhaps I'm just projecting my own concern about it. I know I've never completely freed myself of the suspicion that there are some extremely odd things about this mission. I'm sure you'll agree there's some truth in what I say.

Dr. Dave Bowman: Well, I don't know. That's rather a difficult question to answer.

When we reach this point, there will be no going back. The then newer generation will be asking why keep those dusty old books? Why do a lot of research with pencil and paper? We are joined to the clean, clear, smart Knowosphere and it is us.

The immensity, accuracy and speed of the Knowosphere offer you all kinds of possibilities. You can download a recipe or a book, research an illness, do your banking, or study for a college degree. Then, when all seems to be going well, a great storm cloud appears and you think it is time to run for cover. The threat is artificial intelligence (AI) and its mechanical manifestation, robots.

In addition to the virtually infinite quantity of static information available through the Knowosphere, everyone today must increasingly confront the oncoming wave of artificial intelligence. AI analyzes vast quantities of information and finds patterns to guide people and machines.

You probably are interacting with artificial intelligence more than you think are. For example, airlines use it to lead you through the booking and ticketing process. Online travel planning and booking services are using AI extensively, pioneered by Expedia and heavily used by TripAdvisor. Food stores, discount retail chains, Amazon, and others use AI to make offers tailored to your profile via their constantly updated databases. Credit card companies have very sophisticated AI algorithms to spot probable fraudulent uses of your credit card.

That is good for everybody—the seller, you, and the world at large. But what about an AI machine replacing you?

Everyone can image their job disappearing or their profession becoming obsolete. I thought being an author was safe. Then I read in *Business insider* that Russia published one of the first computer-generated works of fiction in 2008.[44] *True Love* was the work of a computer program and a team of IT specialists. The 320-page novel is a variation of Leo Tolstoy's *Anna Karenina*, but worded in the style of a Japanese author called Haruki Murakami. Here is sample of AI imagination:

> Kitty couldn't fall asleep for a long time. Her nerves were strained as two tight strings, and even a glass of hot wine, that Vronsky made her drink, did not help her. Lying in bed she kept going over and over that monstrous scene at the meadow.

This may not be priceless prose, but the handwriting is on the wall. Eventually, I will be competing with robots for reader market share. Some authors of a continuous stream of blockbuster novels may actually be robots, but that is something I will look into another time! For now, we should look further into artificial intelligence.

What is AI and Where is it Going?

As the world speeds towards seemingly intractable problems such as overpopulation, depleted resources and global warming, we will increasingly need breakthroughs produced by ingenuity and insight. Science claims that Artificial intelligence (AI) is a solution for many of our future needs. What is AI, anyway?

Artificial Intelligence is the ability of a computer or other machine to perform those activities that generally require intelligence. Artificial intelligence devices range from bug-like robots that can find their way around a terrain to mega-computers that someday may be more intelligent than humans are. The use of the term artificial intelligence varies in ways ranging from an engineering and scientific discipline to a specific computer, program or device.

First, let us dispel the startling statements and popular movie themes telling us that artificial intelligence will greatly exceed human intelligence in just a few decades. There may be little doubt that this will probably be the case for applications mostly requiring only massive and repetitive computing, such as data entry, but is not so certain for projects requiring significant amounts of imagination and creativity. In any case, it is highly unlikely that androids will be running around conquering the world, despite what we see in the movies.

AI computers can access very large databases. They are useful in detailed multidimensional design. They can manage vast projects. There is talk of computer-like nanorobots that can circulate around in your body. They can find the location of cancer cells and deliver drugs to disease sites. There are even computer programs to invent new devices. However, as far as I am aware, no computer independently came up with the general theory of relativity.

Increasingly, tiny single purpose computers called micro-processors or embedded systems have replaced electronic logic circuits. These can introduce more intelligence into the control system. Now we take for granted the availability of home controls that not only adjust temperature, but also manage the security system, lock and unlock doors, water the lawn, and remind you to walk the dog. Current models of automobiles all depend on microprocessors for their operation and maintenance. Cars, airplanes, boats, and space vehicles utilize countless simple AI control devices. These devices have an IQ of less than an ant, but the technology has evolved to a high degree of confidence, reliability and low cost.

Complex AI

As artificial intelligence solves problems that are more complex and executes large-scale useful jobs, this will be a payoff for humanity. These challenges could range from diagnosing diseases to managing manufacturing plants. I call this complex AI because complex computers and sophisticated sensors are involved. There will be larger and larger amounts of data, primarily stored in the computer clouds, and there will be software that sharpens its intelligence through continual learning. This can all be part of the Knowosphere.

The wakeup call came when IBM's Deep Blue supercomputer defeated Grandmaster Gary Kasparov in chess in 1997. Deep Blue's per circuit processing speeds are many fold faster than Kasparov's neuron processing speeds. It could examine more than 200 million chess moves per second!

The public really became aware of big AI when IBM's ultra super AI computer, Watson, beat two former winners of the television quiz show *Jeopardy!* Watson received the first prize of $1 million. IBM built Watson's system around massively parallel processors. It uses IBM's *DeepQA* technology to generate hypotheses, gather massive evidence, and continue analyzing the data until it can propose a solution. The system can process 500 gigabytes, the equivalent of a million books, per second. This program generally does not compute exact answers; it searches for the highest probability answer or solution.

In the *Jeopardy!* challenge, Watson used encyclopedias, dictionaries, news sources, literary works and much more as sources. Watson would have to respond to the quiz questions in a few seconds, which at the time, many thought was impossible to do, but the machine clearly succeeded. IBM's first commercial applications of Watson have been mainly in healthcare. With its natural language communications with users, hypothesis generation, and evidence-based learning, it is a natural for use by medical professionals.

Brainlike Computers

Another approach in artificial intelligence is to avoid the use of precisely programmed digital computers and instead make an electronic computer that emulates the neurons and synapses of the brain.[45] The strength of connections between neurons represents the relative strength from associating ideas, places, words, and the like. Experience likely strengthens or weakens these connections This form of computing, sometimes called associative inference or thinking in analogies, is inexact compared to digital computing in standard computers, but it is often much faster, uses much less power, can analyze with very incomplete data, and works despite some damage and noise, or irrelevant information, in its structure.

Since the artificial neuron experiments with simple electronics after World War II, the principles have been widely known. Brainlike computers, often called cognitive computers, are a more recent technology. Stanford University, California Institute of Technology, IBM, and Qualcomm are among the leaders with cognitive computer projects. These computers and others of their kind probably will be the basis for the most general application AI, which will be equivalent to the overall intelligence of large mammals and humans.

In August 2014, IBM announced their brain-inspired computer chip. Called "TrueNorth," this chip has a million neurons—about as many as in the honeybee.[46] It carries out 46 billion synaptic operations per second in its 256 million programmable synapses powered by a hearing aid battery. Its 5.4 billion transistors fit into a space the size of a postage stamp.

An important application for TrueNorth is video pattern recognition. It should be able to recognize people and objects in a scene; do better speech recognition than the present systems, and consequently will likely find an immediate home in smartphones.

It is All about Jobs

Ultimately, the question is about jobs. Everyone from the poorest to the richest is wondering about future unemployment. Very important, from a social stability point of view, is how the future unemployment breaks out in the lowest, middle, and highest income categories. A lot has appeared about this in the press lately with most of the reports tracing their data back to a study in September 2013 at Oxford University.[47] This study used "a novel methodology to estimate the probability of computerization for 702 detailed occupations, using a complex mathematical model they refer to as the 'Gaussian process classifier.'" What woke up the world is their conclusion that 47 percent of the total U.S. employment is at risk of automation over "perhaps a decade or two." They completed the study in England; however, the occupational work data came from the U.S. Department of Labor.

An important point the authors, Carl Benedikt Frey and Michael A. Osborne, make is that "While computerization has been historically confined to routine tasks involving explicit rule-based activities, algorithms for big data are now rapidly entering domains reliant on pattern recognition and can be readily substituted for labor in a wide range of non-routine tasks. In addition, advanced robots are gaining enhanced senses and dexterity, allowing them to perform a broader scope of manual tasks."

Another important point to bear in mind when assessing the "robot threat" is that the acceptance of AI and robots has greatly increased, as more of the machines know how to listen and speak in plain language rather than relying on keyboards, screens, and tedious coding. New applications call for humans and AI or robots to collaborate in tasks. A commonly encountered example of AI/human interaction is the replacement of supermarket cashiers by automatic self-serve checkout stations, although, a human assistant is available to assist at several checkout stations.

Frey and Osborne's model predicts that workers in transportation, logistics, the bulk of office and administrative support workers, and production occupations are at risk. These findings agree with technological developments. They were surprised, however, to find that a substantial number of service jobs are vulnerable to AI and robots. They note that there is a growing market for service robots and declining advantage of human labor in the hitherto safe jobs involving mobility and dexterity.

As *Time's* David Von Drehle puts it, "If your job involves learning a set of logical rules or a statistical model that you apply to task after task—whether you are grilling a hamburger or issuing a boarding pass or completing a tax return—you are ripe for replacement by a robot."[48] Alternatively, maybe you can hang on as a robot's helper like the airline agents who assist using the boarding pass machines.

In any case, workers and potential workers fled factory jobs for the lower paying but supposedly better job stability of, for example, restaurant jobs. In the last half of the 1900s, where I worked in the industrial northeast, labor was shifting from making things to helping other people eat and sleep. Fast food restaurants, motels, and strip-malls moved in to the vacant spaces left by vacated and demolished factories.

However, that was a career choice saving only a generation or two. As Erik Brynjolfsson and Andrew McAfee point out in *Race Against the Machine,* "How can so much value creation and so much economic misfortune coexist? How can technologies accelerate while incomes stagnate? These apparent paradoxes can be resolved by combining some well-understood economic principles with the observation that there is a growing mismatch between rapidly advancing digital technologies and slow-changing humans."[49]

While there is no sure formula for job security, besides acquiring technical, social and computer skills, a person starting out now should be a college graduate if possible. The old saying used to be, "If you can't find a job, join the Army." In January 2014, the U.S. Army made it known that it is considering shrinking the size of the Army's brigade combat teams by a quarter and replacing the soldiers with robots. The Army would like to go from 540,000 soldiers to 490,000 soldiers or less a year or so later. That's at least 50,000 jobs lost.

If robots and AI should take over a substantial percentage of all jobs—even if fewer than the 47% of the Oxford study envisions could happen—they could become a part of the family of organisms closely associated with man. This would be hard to visualize with the clunky machines shown making automobiles. Now that the latest generation of robots has personality, can move around and do things according to what they see, and generally relate to people in sympathetic ways, the idea is not so farfetched. It is not hard to see robots in the workplace or home accepted as living beings identified as one or more species of artificial life.[50]

The public has already accepted this in two movies, *"Robot and Frank"* and *"Her."* In *"Robot and Frank"*, a son gives a personable domestic robot to his father, an aging jewel thief who lives alone. At first, he disparages the robot, but the robot wins Frank over, and they become close friends as the master criminal and his amiable sidekick.

"Her," a more recent movie, shows a lonely young man discovering a virtual woman who is really an AI computer program. They spend time together, explore each other's psyches, and eventually find themselves in love.

These portrayals of robots and AI are subdued, although they show more nuance than the classic science fiction versions portrayed as Hal in *2001: A Space Odyssey* or R2D2 in *Star Wars*. People do not find it strange to buddy up with a robot or computer program if they offer something—especially love and understanding—in return. They could become the new version of pets. Sherry Turkle explores these themes in detail based on her psychological studies of children interacting with robots, noting the present models of buddy robots judged by the children to be "alive enough."[51]

So two things are really going on here, robots are taking over our jobs, and robots are taking over our hearts and minds.

To a certain extent, this has already been happening through the growing dependence on smartphones by some people, particularly the younger generation. People are developing a sense of intimacy and trust with these otherwise inanimate devices of metal, glass and electronics that exceeds that with other people.

Stephen Hawking, Elon Musk, and other big thinkers have expressed concerns that AI could bring about an end to our civilization. I think the cartoon character, Pogo, said something relevant about this: "We have met the enemy and he is us."

We could give up to the machines by default. We are so bound to our computers and their access device, the smart phone, that every advance in information technology leads to reducing our work and lessen our apparent need for thinking. It is not that robots and AI might take over; it is that people might give in.

Where Next

Artificial intelligence presently works for smaller problems with more achievable goals. Successful applications include as mentioned earlier, medical diagnostics, in addition to stock market trading, optimal vehicle control, mineral prospecting and home appliances. At best, there are AI controlled machines that can automatically do limited tasks such as vacuuming a floor or guiding a rocket.

The AI computers and systems up to this point have generally been judged disappointing in terms of mimicking human thought and intelligence. It became clear that artificial intelligence programs were limited in scope because they incorporated systematic computational algorithms based on reductionist conceptions of how to solve problems. The models could not reach out and incorporate new variables or data that the model itself thought might be useful, let alone anything abstract.

Now, however, Deep Learning is the next phase of AI development. Its thinking follows the neural thinking patterns observed in the brain. The deep thinking computer keeps absorbing massive amounts of data related to a task, until it can develop operational patterns and do that task itself. One emerging application is recognizing human and animals by their photographs.

Facebook and Google are experimenting with deep learning for facial recognition and verbal communications, among other areas. Google expects to improve their search engine algorithm by enhancing your search experience with deep learning. Larry Page, Google's cofounder, remarked, "The Ultimate Search Engine is as smart as people—or smarter."

Amazon and Netflix, among other emporiums of the Knowosphere, aid your search for products, books and videos by identifying other similar, products you bought and apparently liked. In other words, your mind feeds information into their mind with each additional search or transaction you make.

6

VIRTUAL REALITY AND ME

Virtual Reality

With the technology developed today, to feel that you are really engaging with the whole world in all its dimensions, you can explore any space in the virtual world sometimes called the metaverse. This is the digital media of virtual reality (VR). In the current versions, you wear a head-mounted display that positions you wherever your imagination takes you. You are a rock climber dangling from a mile high cliff, a blood cell speeding through the pumping heart, a time traveler in the asteroid belt, fighting squads of bad guys in a war game, or maybe a gyrating participant in a frenzied rock concert. The concept is reminiscent of the old 3D movies, but the cardboard and cellophane glasses are now an electronic display connected to an endless computer.[52]

I first explored VR at the Ars Electronica Center in Linz, Austria, which I chanced upon during a Danube river cruise.[53] Ars Electronica is a museum of the future with a focus on the impact of technological developments on society. Besides the interactive exhibits of robots, urban landscapes, and genetic engineering, they have an awesome VR demonstration called Deep Space. I put on special glasses and entered a room half the size of a basketball court. Video projectors sent beams this way and that.

The lights went out, and I found myself underwater. Fish were swimming in front of me, behind me, and above me. Silence reigned. The loud sloshing sound I remember when scuba diving was not there. I was just floating underwater. I reached out and touched a fish.

Then I was a world champion racing skier doing a run up to 90 miles per hour (145 kilometers per hour). Several times, I shot out over an awesome drop and other times I dug my sharpened ski edges into the shattering ice in excruciating and precise turns. This time the extreme motion was a major distraction: because my ears, which are my motion and balance sensors, did not sense my body moving but my eyes did, I suddenly felt disoriented and could not stand up!

What I experienced at Ars Electronica, is the disturbing of the user's balance—a frightening feeling and possibly dangerous outcome. It happens when the user sees motion all around but the motion sensors in the ears do not sense the motion. Some software tricks appear to help. Meanwhile, until this issue is resolved, VR users should participate in the experience sitting instead of standing, as they will stagger helplessly around the room. This is a basic problem with VR.

For the technically inclined, the projection screen was 52 ½ by 29 ½ feet (16 by 9 meters), illuminated at 120 frames per second at 8,192 by 4,320 pixels by eight projectors. This is super high definition 3D imagery.

Some recent 3D movies like *Gravity* (2013), also had high definition and sense of being there, floating around space vehicles and space junk. The Ars Electronica experience, however, made the viewer feel like he or she was in the center of the action and not just an observer.

Indeed, VR seems to appeal most to people who are on a personal quest for satisfaction in a space of their choosing. Video games are by far the most popular VR application as of this writing. In 2015, gaming and entertainment VR ventures raised over $500 million in venture capital investment while all else—architectural/3D visualization, education, social experiences and health care in that order—raised about $100 million, according to VR industry specialist GreenlightVR.com.[54] The future will tell us if this is where society's priorities are, but it certainly does indicate where the profits lie.

The practical problems with VR currently seem to be solvable by new technology and engineering. One problem is the need for the pumping of volumes of digitized information into the display. This requires very wide band data transmission media, which generally consume a lot of energy and are costly. There are a number of proposed solutions. Fiber optic transmission cable and displays can be lighter and cheaper. In a novel approach towards cost reduction, Google is producing cardboard glasses with plastic lenses for viewing VR displayed by your smartphone. These sell for less than $10 from third party sources or you can make your own.[55]

Oculus, a startup purchased by Facebook for $2 billion, is a major player in the infancy of VR business. Their display is large and heavy, but they promise a version the size of sunglasses. Meanwhile, Microsoft is working on a system called HoloLens using holograms. These are 3D images formed from the interference of light beams from a coherent imaging source. This Microsoft development is not total VR where total immersion of the user in the virtual world is required. The HoloLens delivers a mixed reality, or augmented reality (AR), such as changing the color and design of a motorcycle in your room, or an architectural design sitting in the space above your desk. A startup with a promising AR system is Magic Leap. Their board includes representatives from Google and Qualcomm.

Media and technology leaders generally feel that VR, and its variation, AR, is the Next Big Thing after smartphones. Its development is still in the early stages, however, for first adapters. Like television, it will require years to go from crude image boxes to reliable, high-definition, low-cost displays. Like music and videos, it will require years to accumulate libraries of low cost or free programs and apps. Nevertheless, the invasion is underway.

The Imaginarium

Suppose Alice fell down the rabbit hole and landed in a world better than the one she left. She had just put on special glasses and she found herself sky diving into the Grand Canyon. Multicolor canyon walls dropped from the top of the view to way below. A tiny river snaked along the bottom. Whew! That was close! A big hawk just glided by—maybe 20 feet or 7 meters away. Alice thrashed around and shouted, "Where's the ripcord. Please—I'm going to die!"

Alice actually liked the light, attractive 3D glasses she was wearing—much better than the original clunky goggles. As she removed her glasses to avoid certain death in her fall, she noticed the white rabbit standing next to her wearing a cute pair of custom-made rabbit glasses. He went from holding his paws out like wings for gliding in the canyon to putting them over his eyes and collapsing on the ground. He stumbled to his feet, consulted his smartphone time, and announced to no one in particular, "Got to run! Got to run!"

Alice was in a media room, which in some form or other may be in a majority of homes, schools and offices by 2020. I call it an "Imaginarium." A family, a class of students, associates in an office, or attendees at a conference could share an all-surrounding view.

The Imaginarium is a special complete projection of virtual reality for shared, immersive viewing. While conventional VR with Oculus goggles is an amazing experience for individual viewing like gaming, 3D projection is required for a room full of people. 3D projection for the Imaginarium experience is achievable in several different ways.

There could be one or two 3D video projectors, and the images, and one would view scenes through cheap polarized glasses, color filters, or expensive electronic "active" glasses. Each of the current glasses designs has comfort issues, and it may take years for the best design to evolve.

The other approach is to use a flat screen TV, using 3D viewing features built into its electronics. Although not yet heavily promoted, these are available now for either passive or active glasses technology. 3D home television in the U.S. started in 2010 but began a decline in 2013. It has started with conflicting technical standards, cumbersome operating procedures, and very few programs. These have been mainly sports events such as PGA golf and movies. There is a chicken-and-egg problem of producers not willing to invest in expensive 3D programming until there are more viewers, and potential viewers avoiding 3D TV until there are a lot more quality 3D programs.

Large-scale 3D virtual reality home and commercial video is in the technology development curve where color television was in the 1950s. The first nationwide color TV broadcast was in January 1, 1954 for the Tournament of Roses Parade on NBC. However, it was not until fifteen years or so later that many American consumers bought color TV sets, because by then many shows were finally in color and the TV set prices had dropped appreciably. Even then, old timers like me recall that the color viewing was a very fussy procedure to get the right color balance. Faces were often pinkish, and trees were hues of blue-green.

Among customers, there will always be early adopters, fascinated by the technology and/or they enjoy the bragging rights. The 3D room systems will continue to improve until they can provide a virtual reality experience very nearly as good as the real thing.

To produce programs and movies, one needs a "360 degree" camera. In one entry into the field, Google has collaborated with GoPro, a video camera manufacturer, to produce a 360-degree camera array. It is actually sixteen cameras arranged in a circle, facing outward. The estimated price as of mid-2015 is about $15,000. Special software and video editing facilities are also required.

For best image experience, connect the Imaginarium to a very high bandwidth video channel—probably several times the standard broadcast video bandwidth of about three Mbps (megabits per second). While currently quality television uses five Mbps, for the best quality, the ultra-high definition bandwidth of 25 Mbps would be required.

Producing video at locations everywhere on the globe is possible, as Google has shown with Google Maps. They seem to have photographed every house, street, seascape, canyon, and mountain.[56]

So now that you have installed your Imaginarium and you have bought a new set of furniture for viewers comfort, what sort of things can you do?

- Sports events – You will be able to watch football, basketball, tennis, golf and many other sports where you are in the field or court and the players run on all sides around you.
- Culture – You can enjoy a classical symphony from your position next to the conductor. This should get your kids interested in classical music. You could also walk through a famous museum like the Louvre in Paris, stopping at works of art as long as you like.
- Travel – How about riding a gondola through the canals of Venice while the gondolier serenades you with singing "O Sole Mio?"
- Education – The kids can set aside their smartphones and explore forest, underwater corral gardens, anatomy, and historic places, all as if they were right there. With some programs, they can move their phones around in space to explore an entire scene.

Possibly this has warmed the hearts of the cyber industrialists. As Magic Leap says in their mission statement:

> Our whole company...starts with a love for people in general—wanting to bring joy and a sense of magic to everyone...Technology enables us to open up those parts of us we first felt as kids...complete joy and wonder and love of others and the creatures and plants and people all around us.

If any of this vision comes to pass, it will be a great thing. The Imaginarium will not replace our imagination but will be a source that inspires new imagery in our minds. I think a major problem with our educational system is that it often dulls the senses and suffocates the imagination. The Imaginarium and other VR systems offer the possibility to reverse our current slide into intellectual and cultural oblivion.

PART 2

WHAT TO LEARN AND HOW TO THINK IN THE AGE OF GOOGLE

7

DECISIONS

The Destruction of our Attention Span

All of the new digital media including social media, thousands of apps, selfies, and virtual reality can make life more self-satisfying and engaging. They all, however, tend to irrevocably reduce our attention span. We have moved to an instant environment.

Quality, at least in the classic sense, gives way to the "latest thing", the sound bite endlessly rehashed, and the rock concert ever louder. Do many of the younger generation really know or care why a painting or an opera is a masterpiece? They might lose interest quickly upon discovering the time they would have to invest in learning and appreciating the classical arts.

As one who should have great perspective about humanity and the cultural trends, Pope Benedict VXI said, "New technologies and the progress they bring can make it impossible to distinguish truth from illusion and can lead to confusion between reality and virtual reality. The image can also become independent from reality, it can give birth to a virtual world, with various consequences—above all the risk of indifference towards real life." This was in a speech at a world conference of Catholic media in October 2010.

Dr. David Krakauer, president of the Santa Fe Institute, a world leader in the study of complexity, is concerned about what he calls App I, meaning app intelligence. He said in an interview with *Nautilus* magazine, "Let me just give you some examples of this, and it has to do fundamentally with the abdication of free will. It is already the case that for many of us when we make a decision about what book to read or what film to see or what restaurant to eat at, we don't make a reasonable decision based on personal experience, but on the recommendations of an app!"[57]

He went on to say, "I'm not a technology doom and gloom type; I love the stuff. But I am aware that with all the increments in capability are coming decrements in humanity."

In the end, will the digital establishment win because people give in? Will a handful of vendors sell you just what you are looking for as you consult with your smartphone digital assistant? Will the robot-equipped factory keep producing whether you show up for work or not? Such life styles can serve to remind us that we are sliding down the digital rabbit hole into Huxley's *Brave New World*.[58]

Facebook is not waiting for you to make up your mind. At their annual F8 conference for Facebook reps, Mark Zuckerberg, the CEO, said that we're sharing ever more complex experiences—verbal, photos, videos and soon VR—and the natural endpoint is virtual and augmented reality. Michael Abrash, the chief scientist of the Oculus VR subsidiary, declared, referring to the science fiction movie, *Matrix*, "Unlike Morpheus, I'm not offering you a choice of (pills) today. No matter what you pick, we're heading down the rabbit hole together."

To Dive or not to Dive

Diving headlong into the digital rabbit hole is a decision I am very glad I am too old to have to make. If I were a millennial venturing forth today, I would be wise to avoid following the crowd into the digital Knowosphere. I should be strong, think for myself, build a satisfying career, maybe have a good family, and even build an impressive fortune. But, wait a moment! Aren't there too many contingencies here? Anyone could think:

Yes, I should follow the crowd. Why should I try to think through my problems and find my own way? My family is not much help, but my friends are right there on my smartphone. I can talk to them anytime, send Instagrams, or hang out on Facebook. Why knock yourself out?

As for a career, there is no job security anymore. Retirement plan? Forget about it! Maybe it's better to drive an Uber car when I need money—that's driving my own car as if it's a taxi through booking and payment on my smartphone. Then I can enjoy life whenever I feel like it. And, I get to keep my car.

Oh yes, and about the family: Hopefully, I'll find someone on one of the dating sites I cruise. Maybe we'll have a kid or two. They can learn a lot by online education and cruising the Net.

The thinking just expressed is very common in today's society, and represents that "everything's cool" attitude of the '60s flower child generation. Well, everything may not be just fine. Now robotics may be something people have to deal with in many stages of their career. We cannot predict accurately how the future will look in the robotized economy of tomorrow, but we can get a sense of the future through a scenario found in my book, *Winter of the Genomes.*[59] Let us sit in on a job interview in 2050. Our heroine has just graduated from her local community college with a business degree and technology studies. This is her version:

"I found my way through an ordinary looking office to a chair facing a desk and a nattily dressed roboperson sitting behind it. He spoke first, breaking the silence."

"Good morning, Amy," he said, smiling reassuringly. "Can I use your first name? We want you to feel part of our family."

"Yes, sir," I said, fidgeting. This Robot was more imposing than the ones we had to clean the house, cook, and wash the dishes.

"Let me get to our business. We have three job openings that might interest you."

"Oh, what are they?" I said. "I haven't received any summary information."

"The first one on the list is quite physical. You will be trained to remove factory robots that require maintenance, and you will move in substitutes and install them."

"All by myself?"

"Occasionally a handy man will be found to help, but most of the time you will use a helper robot. He can lift 250 kilos (550 pounds)."

"Hmmm. What's the second position?"

"You will assist a team of robots who are servicing cars and light trucks. You know, they are removing and replacing tires, doing lube jobs, and testing and replacing various parts. You will greet customers, help the robots find parts which tend to get scattered around, and help the AI computer order more parts."

"These positions sound interesting, but do you have anything, shall we say, more cerebral?"

"Well, here's one a little different. Do you have some familiarity with electronics and can you do delicate hand work?"

"Yes," I answered attentively.

"There's an opening to apprentice repairing robobees."

"Huh?"

"These fascinating little bugs are about three centimeters long and are programmed to pollinate fruit and vegetable plants and trees. They get banged around a lot, and a skilled technician must constantly replace their delicate wings and other parts. You might even get some free honey." He smiled, quite pleased with his remark.

I thought for what seemed like a long time, and decided to probe further. "Do any of these positions offer a career path, so that I could reasonably hope to run, say, a vehicle repair company or robobee pollination service company some day?"

Robots don't think for extended periods, but this one seemed to be. I guess seconds seemed like minutes to me at this critical point in my job search.

"Well," he said, "we can explore this, but I can't offer much hope. At best, it will be you and the robots in the corporate office. Robots seem to work best when they are managed by robots, and they are not paid. The owners are always looking for the lowest cost solution."

At this point, I felt that even though it might sour the interview somewhat, I should probe once more. "Then after I gain work experience with the robots, I should look for something where I work directly with the owners?"

"Bingo!" he answered. This conversation could become commonplace by 2040.

In summary of earlier parts of this book, the takeover of our minds by digital media will be due in part to these powerful factors: (1) An Internet-based solution is the solution entailing least action or effort, and (2) The selection of Internet services for everything from connecting to social networks to researching deeply technical subjects. The Internet is fast becoming everyone's first choice because that is where all the information and connectivity apparently is. Before you know it, the Internet will be part of you all the time.

The family unit, as a source of information and as the hub of social networking, will continue to decline in importance. People will seek out classmates, the gang, the team, the group and the social connections on the Internet for the protection, support, coaching, education and the transmission of culture that the family used to provide. If this makes you conflicted or unhappy, you can always take a little something that will make you feel all better.

Novelist and futurist Aldous Huxley solved psychological stress problems for the citizens of his *Brave New World*. Their government distributed the *soma* pill, which wiped out negative emotion. You just felt good all the time. The government could do whatever it wanted to do without worrying about your opinion. A character in the book, Mustapha Mond, the World Controller of Western Europe, says, "The world's stable now. People are happy; they get what they want, and they never want what they can't get. They're well off; they're safe; they're never ill; they're not afraid of death; they're blissfully ignorant of passion and old age; they're plagued with no mothers or fathers; they've got no wives, or children, or lovers to feel strongly about; they're so conditioned that they practically can't help behaving as they ought to behave. And if anything should go wrong, there's soma."

Choices

Today's younger generation will face some major choices about their coming lifestyle. Will they have a house? A big place with lawns? A tiny house or mobile home? An apartment? A tiny apartment? A shared living facility—perhaps even lives in their parents' house. When I was at that stage an apartment or a starter house were the predominant choices. You were happy with a refurbished 10-year-old car, a clunky black dial telephone, and possibly the newest thing—a snowy black and white television with a wobbly rabbit ears antenna.

Constraints and opportunities faced by the new entrants into the social economy have drastically changed. Lower real income has revived concepts such as shared living and transportation, and the all-enveloping Internet with its new paradigms of thinking and living have changed everything. Then, there will be the robots.

We will be entering a new world of transition over at least two generations. This will start with the young adults in today's "millennial generation" who are more excited about iPhones and cool social media than about automobiles and big houses. They tend to trust gadgets, apps, and social media more than the retired generation does. We are going through another technological and economic generational cycle.

How well I remember the '50s and '60s; a time of unbounded optimism carried over from winning World War II. Everyone in all walks of life imagined that everything was possible. Breathless releases about new technologies like Picturephones and personal airplanes appeared in *Life* and other family magazines. Lewis Strauss, the Chairman of the U.S. Atomic Energy Commission under President Eisenhower, famously said, "Our children will enjoy in their homes electrical energy too cheap to meter..."

It was a time of anything-is-possible enthusiasm which bubbled over even to excitement about flashy car designs. The tailfins! The chrome! The white sidewalls! The four on the floor! We felt good about life. The buoyant ads of the large American family, all smiling, going to the lake or beach in their "woody" beach wagon reflected the optimism of the times. This is what mattered when I was growing up. This is no longer the case. Now cars are all the same featureless shapes, without excitement or distinction. They are all optimized for fuel economy and low cost. That is not a bad thing but they are not very thrilling. In addition, robots make them. Soon robots will drive them.

Recently, out of nowhere came the smartphones, which serve as our portal to our friends and connect us to the Knowosphere worldwide. All that matters now is our lifeline of connection to everyone and everything.

The Digital Divides

People's involvement with the Knowosphere will vary a lot depending where they find themselves in society's socio-economic strata. Ultimately, the involvement with the Knowosphere and intensity of use of the Internet may well have a lot to do with a person's social class and income. While the smartphone does not represent an escape hatch from the poverty, without it, a person has almost no hope of escape. A smartphone can provide access to basic education courses, information and job search, sports reports, banking, news and meeting on or offline with friends. If a young adult cannot read effectively and is only minimally computer literate, then he or she is already in danger of marginalization from the digital world.

Health and medicine are extremely important areas that can be vastly improved using smartphones.[60] The largest impact could be for the poor. A number of websites that provide lists of possible diseases or health conditions based on symptoms. You simply type your symptoms directly into the smartphone, tablet, or computer search bar for a diagnosis. Some are online health information sites like WebMD, and some are health information websites of institutions like the Mayo Clinic and government agencies.

You type in or speak your symptoms and the sites are displayed which will offer suggestions to your problem. They can save costly visits to doctors and hospitals. With health records digitized and stored in the Knowosphere, and if you allow these sites access to your health file, the medical sites could be correspondingly more helpful to you.

Another emerging application of smartphones, smartwatches, and other "wearables," is transmission of data to monitoring services of your clinically important variables. These include blood sugar, especially for diabetics, heart rate and blood pressure, exercise information, and ambient concerns like carbon monoxide levels. There are of course many other health-related uses of the Internet including advisories about infant care, alarms from the elderly living alone, and food and diet advisories including local sources of healthy food. Online, automated mental health diagnostics is a current area of product development.

While all levels of society can use these Internet-based health services, the poor and disenfranchised would find the greatest life changing consequences because they may have nowhere else to turn.

People in the middle class who use advanced digital technologies are likely to increase their knowledge, life satisfaction, and job advancement compared with the poorer classes stuck with just their smart phones and occasional laptops. This is a constant problem with productivity technology. The new technology can help everybody but without access, the poor do not benefit as much as those in the middle and upper economic classes.

Some of those in the middle class who still have employment have enough additional income and presumably job security so that its members can indulge in expensive pastimes like complex and expensive video games. A Microsoft Xbox console costs over $300. The more ambitious middle class can enroll in online courses, some for college credit. The major investment, out of reach for the poor, would include a quality computer system with one or more large screen displays, a good printer for spewing out important reference documents, and premium high-speed Internet service. The benefits pile up. Such an ambitious student could also use his or her computer system for managing investments and researching and booking overseas vacations.

With money and leisure time come more digital goodies. One promotion as the "Next Big Thing" is, of course, virtual reality (VR). Don an audio-video headset and your rabbit hole drops you into a bar where you sit next to your Facebook friends and walk around among them, not just see their faces on a screen. If it is a sports bar, everyone can watch a football game with the players crunching into each other on all sides of the friends in the bar. Some pundits are proclaiming that virtual reality will be better than actuality.

The other "Big Thing" is the Internet of Things (IOT). In technical terms, this is equipment and devices controlled by sensor and all of them, possibly everywhere in the world, and of all kinds, digitally connected. Google is experimenting with connecting thermostats, smoke and gas detectors, and security cameras so that they are self-adjusting and report their results to you on your smartphone. General Electric is developing systems to connect you with your washer, drier, oven, refrigerator and more, when these appliances are not blissfully running themselves. When you head towards the refrigerator, the refrigerator sees you coming, opens, and offers you a beer so that you can effortlessly return to your lounge chair and, immersed in a virtual reality, watch football or play a war game.

In other words, you will not be able to avoid immersing yourself in the digital realm. It will get you, one way or another, until, surrounded, you just go with the flow.

From a socioeconomic point of view, the real problem arises from what the wealthy will do—at least those who own or manage profitable businesses. While they appreciate and use the various digital technologies everyone else uses, additionally, they are likely to increase the productivity of their businesses by using artificial intelligence, robots, Internet services, the Internet of Things and almost anything to reduce troublesome and expensive payrolls.

In short, everyone must get more involved with the Knowosphere, the Internet, and automation just to stay where they are. In order to better themselves, wherever they are in society, people cannot stand still. They must invest in the health and education of themselves and their families. Digital media and services will be a basic resource for people to advance their lives.

NEW THINKING IN THE DIGITAL AGE

A s we have seen, with every passing day, more information piles up in the Knowosphere, preserved forever. People rarely use traditional media to save information anymore. Studying, memorization, and research are giving way to doing online research when required. The rationalization arises, "Is it really so bad if we prefer cyber sources to paper sources?"

The enormous, ever growing, and instantly accessible knowledge base accessed through Google, Microsoft, Yahoo, Amazon and others, what I call the Knowosphere, is so fast and comprehensive that it is a new resource and not just an electronic library. It has information that is required to refocus and refine the individual's thinking, thereby multiplying their mental powers manifold times. Consider creativity. Sitting all by themselves, the computer clouds will not invent anything, and sitting all alone, the individual might not realize his or her full potential as an inventor. However, the combination of the two can produce an invention of immense scope and importance.

We can illustrate the Knowosphere from your perspective by the three-ring Venn diagram below. It shows how to visualize your mind in the always-connected world.

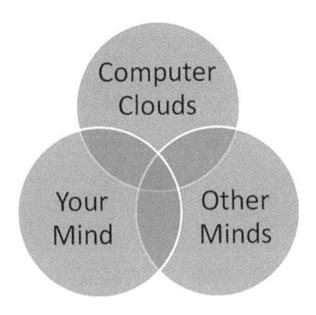

Where will you position your mind?

For example, if total immersion in the digital world is who you are, more of your mind will greatly overlap with the Computer Clouds circle. If you do not care for frequent communications with other people, your mind will not greatly overlap the Other Minds circle. Before computers, you would talk to friends over coffee or tea and visit the library. In the earliest days of mankind, you would have learned through sages and tales passed on through tribal gatherings.

Suppose you do not want to live in an artificial environment, or run with the digital herd? This will be increasingly difficult to do—essentially civil disobedience—but it should always be possible. It would appear that we have constructed a knowledge nirvana, and all we need to do is drift along interacting with it as if we were driving a car and watching the scenery go by. That is what happened to Alice when she and her smart-phone dropped down the digital rabbit hole.

If humans combine with the Knowosphere as an enhanced species, then we have an entangled, adaptive network of humans and machines. Human intelligence will go from how one thinks alone during a complex challenge, and more to how you make the most of the Knowosphere whenever and however you think. They would measure this by an online intelligence test that analyzes you and the Internet working together. Testing candidates who are not computer literate need not apply.

The Mind Merging With the Internet

Exactly how the mind merges with the Internet is not important here unless, in interacting with the Internet, something happens. An interesting study affirmed that something does happen. "Searching the Internet for explanatory knowledge creates an illusion whereby people mistake access to information for their own personal understanding of the information" in the words of Matthew Fisher, Mariel K. Goddu, and Frank C. Keil in the American Psychological Association's *Journal of Experimental Psychology.*[61]

These authors, from the Department of Psychology at Yale University, go on to say that, people become accustomed to carrying out cognitive tasks on the Internet. The study included nine experiments with 152 to 302 participants. They were to research questions including "How does a zipper work?" and "Why are cloudy nights warmer?"

When the study participants remember how to find the information, or their smartphone finds it in partnership with their search engine, then they become less accustomed to remembering the information themselves. This leads to the new mode of learning, which relies ever more on using search and analysis apps on the Internet and ever less on finding, synthesizing and analyzing information from several sources, constituting research.

Fisher, Goddu, and Kiel go on to propose, "The cognitive systems may well be in place for users to treat the Internet as functionally equivalent to an all-knowing expert in transactive memory systems." If true, this is interesting and disconcerting. I think this means that the psychological mechanism is there, so we could well lose whatever interest we had in seeking out the truth. The Internet is the all-knowing expert. How can we do better than that?

Fisher commented, "People must be actively engaged in research when they read a book or talk to an expert rather than searching the Internet." He went on, "If you don't know the answer to a question, it's very apparent to you that that you don't know, and it takes time and effort to find the answer. With the Internet, the lines become blurry between what you know and what you think you know."

"The growing use of smartphones may exacerbate this problem because the Internet search is always within reach," Keil said, "and the effects may be more pronounced when children who are immersed in the Internet from an early age grow up to be adults."

Indeed, the authors write, "for these reasons, the Internet might become even more easily integrated with the human mind than other external sources of knowledge and perhaps even more so than human transactive memory partners, promoting much stronger illusion of knowledge." In lay terms, "If you habitually searched the Internet for information, you will rely less on books and people for knowledge, and you will be fooling yourself about how much you really know."

As for me, by way of full confession, I do the majority of my book research these days on the Internet.

Many Minds and the Internet: Collective Intelligence

People are increasingly turning to collective intelligence to tackle large and pressing problems. The team approach to problem solving goes back to the beginning of civilization. My book, *MegaMinds*, discusses the team approach throughout history.[62] During World War II, the Manhattan Project developed the atomic bomb and considered the prototypical successful large team development. The Knowosphere, however, is raising this approach to a new level.

John Barrow, English physicist and mathematician, writes in *The Guardian*:[63]

> We as a species have entered a new phase of evolution with the appearance of the World Wide Web. You can find out almost anything you want to know at the click of a button, and this happened suddenly, nobody predicted it. This is a collectivization of human information. Once you start to act with other people, you can do things you couldn't do as an individual. You become a connected intelligence and just like joining computers together, that increases your effectiveness and power… For scientists, it means the world is now one giant research group.

With the advent of Internet forums, wikis, research groups, and blogospheres, we have embraced much broader forms of problem solving and innovation. For scientists, the Internet is now a communal research group. This learning and group communication mode known as "collective intelligence" and "crowd-sourced innovation." In its most general form, it is determining the consensus of many minds to find a response to a complex challenge. For example, finding solutions for many problems engendered by climate change is a perfect use for collective intelligence.

The MIT Center for Collective Intelligence has been shepherding the development of an online forum called the Climate Collaboratorium.[64] It will be a constantly evolving computer model of the Earth's atmosphere and human systems with inputs from online scientific chat rooms. All the variables and factors that are imaginable related to climate, the environment, interactions with human beings, and ecology are included in the evolving model.

Professor Thomas W. Malone, the center's founding director and MIT Professor of Management, compares the Collaboratorium to the Manhattan Project. "The difference between the Climate Collaboratorium and the Manhattan Project is that this is a problem everyone in the world needs to solve, but because of new technologies like the Internet, it's possible to enlist far more people than during World War II."[65]

Malone's climate project is formally known as the "Climate CoLab." As of late 2014, it has over 15,000 registered members from more than 150 countries. Their organizations include NASA, the World Bank, the Union of Concerned Scientists, leading universities, businesses, government agencies, and student organizations.

There are of course many examples in the history of collective intelligence that has gone wrong. Contrary to the then prevailing wisdom we now know that the world is not flat and it is not at the center of the solar system. Propaganda with skewed or falsified information for the purpose of inflaming emotions has triggered civil and world wars.

There are however plenty of examples that could be cited to show the amazing accuracy possible with collective intelligence. Malone and his associates at the MIT Center for Collective Intelligence report:[66]

- *Kasparov v. the World* was a chess match held in 1999, when world champion Gary Kasparov played against "the world," with the world's moves determined by majority vote over the Internet of anyone who wanted to participate. Kasparov eventually won, but he said it was the hardest game he ever played (at least until he met IBM's "Big Blue" super computer and lost).
- *NASA Clickworkers.* In 2001-2002, NASA let anyone look at photos of the surface of Mars on the Internet and identify features they thought were craters. Crater locations were designated by sets of coordinates in two-dimensional space. When the coordinates contributed by amateurs were averaged, they were found to be just as accurate as the classifications made by experts.

Another approach to innovation and design using the flexibility and outreach of the Web is to broadcast a request for an invention or design to anyone who cares to rise to the challenge. This is a good example of crowd-sourced innovation. There is a reward to the winner of the challenge—usually in the 10's of $1,000s. A leader in offering this type of service is InnoCentive based in Waltham, Mass.[67] It is a global Web community enabling scientists, engineers and others to collaborate to deliver breakthrough solutions for innovative R&D-driven organizations. Since 2001, their clients have included Procter & Gamble, Eli Lilly, The Rockefeller Foundation, government agencies and non-profits.

As of early 2009, 814 challenges had been posted (a "challenge" is a request for an innovative solution), for which 12,529 solutions have been proposed, and 391 were accepted and received cash awards. Among the challenge solutions that InnoCentive feels are of broad significance are:

- *Oil Spill Recovery.* In 2007, the Oil Spill Recovery Institute posted three challenges dealing with oil spill recovery. One of these was solved later that year by a researcher who proposed a solution based on his expertise in the concrete industry. Insights can be found unpredictably in unrelated applications.
- *Towards eradication of tuberculosis.* Also in 2007 the TB Alliance, a not-for-profit development partnership dedicated to accelerating the discovery and development of drugs to treat TB posted a challenge on the InnoCentive web site to simplify the manufacturing process of a current drug. Solutions were provided by solvers, one of whose mother was a victim of the disease.
- *Clean water in Africa.* A **water filtration system** has been developed in response to a change that uses carbonized coconut shells to filter out large particles and heavy metals. An ultraviolet LED powered by a solar panel then sterilizes the water.

Now the question arises: where would the visionary thinker, the Thomas Edison, fit into this entire comforting new world of collective intelligence? Edison did the best he could without the benefit of Web-based collaborative intelligence, Google or wikis. He achieved much the same thing by surrounding himself with an army of engineers and technicians, and by maintaining his own large technical library. He also gained venturesome technical insights from his social associations with such industrial entrepreneurs as Henry Ford and Harvey Firestone.

Many people would consider all of this prohibitively expensive and time-consuming to do today. They would reach for their laptops and see if solutions are available there.

Leonardo da Vinci, were he alive today, would probably join Internet chat groups and log into the computer clouds in addition to keeping a close circle of friends at his workshop. He would eagerly pick from the nearly infinite number of creative challenges presented to him daily. Leonardo would agree that with our Web incorporating billions of websites and quadrillions of pieces of information, with access to all by a laptop computer, that this data and computing cloud is closer to his infinite universe than simply being able to see the outer limits of the actual universe.

Leonardo's practical nature would undoubtedly appreciate that the use of modern communications technology and the Internet is more efficient, and he would not waste time on inventions that already exist.

Google and the other computer clouds offer a new paradigm of creative thinking. The complex and critical problems confronting civilization today are demanding solutions at a much less leisurely pace than in the past. Darwin could arrive at his theory of evolution over a lifetime with no contrary consequences of his slow, methodical progress.

Today, however, problems including global warming, food and water, and the tightly coupled national economies require genius-level insights in a short time. For these particular problems, if the right solution does not appear in time for implementation, the world system may have crossed the Tipping Point beyond which the system cannot recover.

Thinking for Yourself

Do not confuse the collective intelligence discussed in the previous chapter with the much more commonly encountered "crowd wisdom." People tend to believe that the truth is where the crowd is. The crowd gains an emotional energy from reaffirming its commonly held truth. Another way of looking at this phenomenon is that you will believe in something if a relative, trusted friend, or acknowledged authority believes it. The shared belief will help everyone who trusts you to link up and become a crowd.

The particular belief snowballs in its area of acceptance by everyone, and the group feels cohesive and united. You can readily see this in Facebook posts where friends and followers of a person quickly chime in with "likes" and supportive comments. Many people comment positively to support the group through encouraging the person who just posted. The posting person could have said, "I just read that the ocean is gradually turning pink," and comments could have been, "Wow!" "Awesome!" "Yeah, I also just read that," "Heard it's going to be on CNN."

Such cyber group cheerleading can also be found in LinkedIn groups, Twitter followings, popular blogs and other social media sites. In a sense, this usually is harmless (a notable exception is when teenagers pile on to denigrate an unpopular out-of-the-group kid, otherwise known as Cyber bullying) and frequently relatively unknown talent use it to promote themselves. You should constantly remind yourself that the crowd wisdom requires some skepticism. Just because everyone says it, does not make it true.

Many people have gravitated to the web for news and information. They peruse the websites and blogs ranging from *The New York Times* to perhaps the blog of an obscure devotee of urban honeybees. Online reporting is problematic due to the requirement of the condensed and edited snippets or sound bites to accommodate the small screen devices, especially smartphones. Also, reporters and editors know that people, especially the younger generations, have very short attention spans. Readers are accustomed to one-to-three sentence text messages, and even as they read the news snippet, they have to check additional incoming text messages. Therefore, smart-phone "news" readers should realize that all of the editing might have removed the complete truth in order to fit on the smartphone screen.

Suppose on your palm-size smartphone screen, this caught your attention:

Women who ate fish 5 times a week cut their risk of dying from a heart attack by half.
This statement implies a causal mechanism, but that was not the case. The reporter drafted:
Frequent fish consumption was associated with a 50% reduction in the relative risk of dying from a heart attack.
Her editor's reaction? "Slash. Too wordy, too passive."
The Editor's rewrite?
Women who ate fish five times a week cut their risk of dying later from a heart attack by half.
This edit seems fair enough or is it?

The change streamlines the message, but with a not-so-obvious, unintended cost to the meaning. Was the subject fish consumption responsible for their dying less frequently from heart attacks? The new wording suggests that is the case, but the original study does not support a conclusion of cause and effect.

The foregoing was written by Mark Zweig, MD, and Emily DeVoto, PhD, for *Health News Review*.[68] They suggest the following report using language to be as factually correct as possible:

> *Compared to women who rarely ate fish, those who ate fish regularly had less heart disease and related death. But, this type of study, which just observes people, rather than randomly assigning them to eat fish or not, cannot prove that fish consumption has a protective effect.*

I often take a snippet of interest gleaned from my small tablet and explore it in detail in more technical sites found by a search on my larger home computer. I find that if I encounter an intriguing health snippet online, and after fact checking it, taking into account all the other factors I can think of, it still appears of concern, then I discuss it with my doctor. If he or she finds this syndrome may apply to me, then I know I have probably found an important truth about my health and my doctor benefits also.

What I am leading up to is that we should revisit the DIKW pyramid discussed in chapter three. Starting at the bottom of the pyramid, we could say that the data recorded in some field of study has produced information. This chunk of information is what we see fingering through news releases, blog snippets, and info web pages in our smartphone. Our approach should always be to analyze the information in terms of what else we know and can find to produce reliable knowledge.

This is the beginning of raising ourselves above machines and above people mired in the Web. Then we can synthesize all our knowledge against all known experience that we can gather over all time, and we finally may reach the exalted pinnacle called wisdom.

ADVANCEMENT, EDUCATION, AND CREATIVITY

Suppose everyone in the whole world who was literate in a major language and was skilled in using a dedicated computer decided to learn as much as possible by interacting with the Internet. They would find at least two hours a day to attend online courses, pursue ideas wherever they might lead, discuss issues with friends and mentors, and develop non-Net outside research and projects.

For the most part, this is achievable now. So why is everyone not advancing themselves to the next level of jobs, income, and possibly social advancement? Probably there are many answers, but an obvious and important one is that many people are more concerned with their perceptions of themselves now, and not a new self which may not happen and which might remove them from their family and friends.

I know this from personal experience. I managed a high tech manufacturing company in the greater New York area. I had a standing offer to my employees that if they wanted to study work-related courses in night school, the company would pay their tuition. It turned out that the bottom-rung assembly line workers were the least likely to accept my offer.

One day I asked a bright and promising man who lived in a very poor neighborhood why he had not shown any interest in my offer. Squeezing out a pained smile, he said, "I tried once, but my friends and everyone made fun of me, and they got hostile. As I was walking along, they would circle around me and say stuff like, 'Are you too good for us? We don't want to see you with any books no more.'"

When I left a small country town school after sixth grade to go to a private college preparatory school, I ran into some of the same reaction from some of the other kids. They would say, "Aren't we good enough for you?" Perhaps many people have to deal with this "group versus self" problem one way or another. The easy thing to do is to stick with your group and forget about further advancement.

Now, by going down the digital rabbit hole into Cyberland, you can find a mirror you can ask if you are the fairest one of all. No need to spend weeks, months, or years struggling through an endless expanse of knowledge with little chance you will use what you find or, if you do use it, you will be any happier.

Nevertheless, the Internet and all the associated services are an absolutely essential resource—maybe even the most important information technology developed in the last hundred years. However, for many people, the most important uses of the Internet are social media, shopping, and games. This digital divide will continue to grow ever wider as the Knowosphere becomes the most important resource for most managers, engineers, scientists, students, teachers, writers and creative professionals. It is hard to imagine how we got along without the Knowosphere or what would happen if it collapsed.

Cyberland Delusion

The change in environment for everyone, no matter what their involvement with the Internet, will be that they will find themselves in the age of external knowledge. It will be easier to find what information you are looking for somewhere in the Knowosphere rather than asking your parents, learning from a teacher or associate, or researching through piles of books. Parents, teachers, and books will not be obsolete, but they will serve different roles and functions.

Consequently, I predict that the thinking of the newer generations will tend to be less rigorous because there will be fewer opportunities to cross check hypotheses and theories. They will be doing more of their knowledge development alone. This is not necessarily bad in all cases. It may be better to pursue some knowledge, however wobbly, than no pursuit at all.

Neil Postman (1931-2003), a cultural and media theorist wrote about this in his classic *Amusing Ourselves to Death: Public Discourse in the Age of Show Business.*[69] He was referring mostly to television, because the Internet was new when he wrote, but he presciently said: "Everything from telegraphy and photography in the nineteenth century, to the silicon chip in the twentieth, has amplified the din of information, until matters have reached such proportions today that for the average person, information no longer has any relation to the solution of problems."

On the other hand, the newer generations must learn to use critical thinking as a routine. They must review the information presented to them, consider all the points of view, and do further research if the received information seems biased or incomplete. They must always be skeptical of purported truths.

Mr. Postman also interpreted Aldous Huxley's *Brave New World*, the almost century-old forecast about the coming culture.[70] He said that Huxley thought that the truth would drown in a sea of irrelevance. There would be those who would give us so much information that we would become passive and egotistical.

Many of the young people of the upcoming generation are extensions of the characters in songs, movies and video games. To them, it is easier and more fun to absorb the programming of digital media, movies and concerts than it is to accumulate a lifetime of micro experiences that would become the basis of a valuable person. If they give up life's learning opportunities, they will have given up the possibilities to be biologists, astronomers, rocket engineers, schoolteachers and countless other professions. For those trapped in virtual reality, real reality is no longer a frightening concept. There is no need for confrontation, one can easily deny and block out the unpleasantness. When there is a mega crisis such as someone trying to conquer the world yet again, will anyone care?

A major problem in households as well as in an active democracy is whether people lose interest in the truth or even how to find it. If information satisfies their mind by confirming what they generally think about issues, or just makes them feel good, why take the time and effort to see if there is deception, misinformation or misunderstanding involved?

With the enveloping influence of social media, this problem becomes worse. In the pre-media era, people relied on their family and friends to confirm or deny their concerns when thinking through an issue. These people could advise you, console you, steer you to other people or information sources who might know more.

Now you and your gang on Facebook can share pictures and stories that feel good. There is nothing wrong with that, if done in moderation, but for many people it becomes an obsession. They have a continual quest to satisfy egoism and narcissism. They have a self-imposed pressure for approval online. They want to socialize and fit in. There is the ever-lurking FOMO, fear of missing out.

The Individual, the Internet, and the Truth

The creative person seeks something more than being part of a computer cloud-based social affinity group. He or she increasingly will have to balance plugging into the computer clouds and collective wikis on one hand and, on the other hand, continuing the search for the unexpected that may not be in the clouds. There is the balance between the insightful mind and the collective intelligence. There are the different worlds of the instant other reality on the Internet versus the very long, private intellectual quest. There is the abstract thinking mind versus the ever-improving machine learning.

Therefore, the creative person seeking new truths and models must constantly try to sort out the relevance of the computer cloud information versus what he or she thinks independently. People immersed in information analysis must increasingly be on guard that rumor and invective may be outpacing the quest for the truth.

The industrial revolution has given way to the knowledge revolution. The computer clouds may overwhelm the evolving mind of man. The combination of peoples' minds and clouds' minds, by their very nature, form a super mind. A growing problem however will be that our thinking may not be so focused towards complete analysis and the best analytical methods. Broad-brush holistic solutions to problems perceived in megadata can lead us to new insights, but they can also lull us into overlooking the simpler analyses of the classical scientific method.

Noted MIT computer scientist Joseph Weizenbaum (1923-2008) seemed unimpressed by the Internet and troubled by the fact that it was easy for people to mistake pattern matching for true understanding.[71] For the individual human trying to make the most of the Internet, maintaining perspective about the apparent truth emerging from the data analysis will be very difficult. One way to do this is by seeking perspective through original research.

All over the world people are sensing that knowledge and information have become a common resource and tool, and that has led to whole new Web services, "social media" such as Facebook and Twitter, and Web-based mega companies such as Google and Amazon. Collective thinking, however, can lead to mantras based on questionable science.

Therefore, anyone finding newly discovered "scientific" revelations and other discoveries on the Internet should be skeptical. Scientific detachment would indicate to wait for some time to pass, seek other opinions, and search for probing questions to test the validity of the new and often popular theory. Use the Internet and other resources to find opposite points of view or broader perspectives about the issue.

Imagination and creativity, integrity, a sense of wonder and truth, persistence of inquiry—these keep us above both the turmoil and herd mentality of the Internet. They allow us to profit from the inexhaustible information resource of the Internet if we keep our sense of perspective and good judgment.

Breaking Loose: Imagination and Creativity

With the development of the Worldwide Web, all written information that is interconnected is one resource. Apparent answers become so easily accessible that imagination and invention would cease to be worthwhile. With the absorption of the new generation of younger people with formative minds, by virtual reality and standardized information formats, imagination may wither away.

To create new art and make new discoveries in science, our imaginations must break loose from the Knowosphere at least occasionally. As Albert Einstein wrote:

> The most beautiful experience we can have is the mysterious. It is the fundamental emotion which stands at the cradle of true art and true science. Whoever does not know it and can no longer wonder, no longer marvel, is as good as dead, and his eyes are dimmed.

Thinking more in terms of today's Knowosphere, the noted mathematician and computer scientist, Gregory Chaitin, wrote in *Proving Darwin: Making Biology Mathematical*[72]

> To survive, a society needs to impose coherence, but not too much, lest it do away with creativity altogether. It is a delicate balance, of permitting some individuals to break the rules, up to a point. We are clearly going in the wrong direction now in some societies where creativity is micromanaged by gigantic bureaucracies.
>
> In my view, our most urgent task today is to be creative enough to design a flexible society, a society in which

creativity is somehow tolerated, not like Aldous Huxley's *Brave New World*, which eliminated art and intelligence in favor of stability

The answer of course is education, be it in the home environment or in the schools. It is always with the new generation that we can start fresh.

The child still has the almost naïve capability of unfettered imagination. Some people, very few, keep this imaginative ability through adulthood. Their imaginings leads to inventions, art, designs and explorations of many frontiers never seen before. Emotion is part of this creative formula, and perhaps the emotional element is what is hardest to reconcile in equating the human mind to an advanced computer.

Children and adults must develop the habits of exploration, creativity and life-long learning. In addition, they must develop a sense of truth as an intellectual discipline, and never lose sight of pursuing it.

From this starting point, we can arrive at the three modes of the intellectually stimulated mind: imagination, creativity and invention. With imagination, we can see beyond mere recollection or simple association. It gets us beyond the here and now. The mind's eye projects to another point in space or time. Without complete data or information, the mind creates a mental picture or vision.

Creativity moves forward from imagination to solving a problem or creating a work of art without a complete set of instructions or a recipe. Creativity uses imagination to make an appealing or useful whole from a set of components that would not appear at first glance, to be useful for the job.

Invention carries this process forward farther still. It cycles through imagination, creativity, and experimentation powered by persistence to develop a new product or process.

We must inculcate the value and methods of good research in our student population. As they enter the enterprise world, be it public or private, profit or non-profit, they must have and maintain a critical attitude towards information, knowledge, truth, creative ideas, invention, flights of fancy and imagination. They must realize that the pursuit of new scientific insights have to include focusing on finding truth among all the information and not just processing the information itself. Without the sense of the importance of empirical truth, the relevance of reality is lost and progress stalls.

PART 3

ESCAPE FROM THE
RABBIT HOLE

10

THE INTERNET AND
THE PEOPLE

The growing Internet brain, nurtured by the limitless Knowosphere, and tunneled into by countless personal rabbit holes, is simply a tool and not an end in itself. We must use it with care and use it for our genuine advancement. Many observers of the digital culture say there is an erosion of human values, and I will elaborate on this theme later in this chapter.

I was struck when my grandson in his early 20s—probably a typical millennial—announced apropos of nothing, "I have found a philosophy. I follow Sartre." I could not get a clear idea of his understanding of Sartre's ideas or his famous philosophy of existentialism, but my grandson was clear that the individual is the center of his world. This is me-ism again. The new denizens of Cyberland, having played thousands of video games and texted to infinity, but not yet found satisfying occupations, may be searching for meaning. They seem to be unable to find the traditionally sustaining structure of human values.

We are looking at a festering development. Carl Sagan (1934-1996) the preeminent astronomer who was just entering the digital age, said, "I have a foreboding of an America in my children's or grandchildren's time when… our critical faculties in decline, unable to distinguish between what feels good and what's true, we slide, almost without noticing, back into superstition and darkness..." Sagan goes on to say we will be dealing with a kind of celebration of ignorance.[73]

Sherry Turkle, in her recent book, *Reclaiming Conversation: The Power of Talk in a Digital Age*,[74] adds the technological dimension: "It's not that we have really invented machines that love us or care about us in any way, shape or form, but that we are ready to believe that they do. We are ready to play their game."

There has always been a traditional culture to fall back on, whether in home, schools and churches, but now these institutions seem to be fading. People turn to the Internet. A Pew Research survey found that by mid-2015, only 15% of U.S. adults do not use the Internet, down from 48% in 2000.[75] In the space of less than a generation, we have made the transition to a digital society. Of course, not all of the 85% of the population on the Internet are succumbing to the machines, but the residuals of the paper-only society are withering away.

As stated in the Introduction, the momentum towards a captivating digital society bears restating here:

- Technology – The perpetual digital connection to everything, which can provide us an easy apparent answer, rather than make us devise one of our own.
- Human nature – We gravitate towards convenience, good enough, emotional feedback, least action, and distractions.

We are sliding down the rabbit hole into the digital Cyberworld with no apparent escape. No one can limit himself or herself to just Facebook, VR, video games, online dating, or limitless online research. We must accept that as Eric Schmidt, the Great Helmsman of Google (now Alphabet, Inc.) informs us, "The Internet will be part of your presence all the time."[76] It will be everywhere—invisible but life supporting—like the air we breathe, only presumably more trustworthy.

Were you listening to me? Shut off your smartphone!

The Erosion of Human Values

We are heading toward a digital world. It probably does not matter exactly when. The important thing is to recognize and accept its historic inevitability. Then we can move on and examine the consequences.

This is different from the book age when anyone could opt out of books. The digital age envelops us and forces us to engage whether we like it or not.

For centuries, there were the literate few who carried out the administrative, intellectual, professional, religious, and supervisory functions. The illiterate tended to hold positions in service jobs and manual labor. Now almost all jobs require some digital literacy and ability with digital devices.

People will increasingly divide into two camps: those who are intelligently digital and those who are routinely digital. The digitally intelligent use digital devices from smartphones to communications satellites and so on, as the basis of new enterprises, to further their education and other advancements. An example of development by intelligently digital people for intelligently digital people is Uber, the very successful ride sharing service, which is an alternative to taxis. Uber uses digital technology in all aspects of its operation, from use of the customer's smartphone to call the ride vehicle, give his or her location, and provide credit card information, to settling the accounts of the driver and the company.

The balance of the population, the people who are routinely digital, will mainly use their smartphones for social media access, entertainment, purchases, banking, and other daily routines.

As Jonathan Franzen pointed out in his *New York Times* review of Sherry Turkle's *Reclaiming Conversation: The Power of Talk in a Digital Age*:

> Digital Technology is capitalism in hyperdrive, injecting its logic of consumption and promotion, of monetization and efficiency, into every waking minute.
>
> It is tempting to correlate the rise of "digital democracy" with steeply rising levels of income inequality, to see more than just an irony. But maybe the erosion of human values is a price that most people are willing to pay for the "costless" convenience of Google, the comforts of Facebook and the reliable company of iPhones.[77]

"Digital democracy" may be a contributor to the declining interest in classical music. Slate.com in an in-depth report on this, comments, "When it comes to classical music and American culture, the fat lady hasn't just sung, Brünnhilde has packed her bags and moved to Boca Raton."[78] Among the causes, the author, Mark Vanhoenacker, cites is "the Internet-driven democratization of cultural opinion."

He goes on to say that Sirius XM, the online and satellite radio system, has 9 jazz channels and 20 Latin channels, but only 2 traditionally classical channels. One, called Symphony Hall, has 3,500 Facebook likes, while their DJ Tiesto-curated channel for rock, trance, experimental and electronic music has 89,000 likes.

In his book, *Changing the Subject: Art and Attention in the Internet Age*, Sven Birkerts summarizes that "Fewer young people

THE INTERNET AND THE PEOPLE

are choosing to study the humanities. Fewer great works of art are being produced. There is a real risk of individuality being submerged in the system."[79]

In *Fractured Times: Culture and Society in the Twentieth Century*, Eric Hobsbawn reports that as of 2014 the core live classical music public in New York City is no more than 20,000 people. They represent a mere one quarter of one percent of the city's 8.4 million population.[80]

However, a ray of hope emerges for this discouraging trend and, ironically, it comes from virtual reality. The Los Angeles Philharmonic Orchestra is experimenting with using VR to give you the sensation that you are the sole audience of a grand performance. You are standing right next to the conductor.

Jessi Hempel writes in *Wired* Magazine:[81]

And as I've tested applications of VR and its fraternal twin, augmented reality, over the past year, I've seen remarkable simulations. I stood on the moon with Microsoft's HoloLens. I perched in the forest as Reese Witherspoon wandered by in the movie *Wild*...But no programming has moved me as much as four minutes of classical music put together by the Los Angeles Symphony Orchestra's crack digital initiatives team.

The Los Angeles Symphony VR production opens with Beethoven's Fifth Symphony. The public demonstration will take place in a yellow van named VAN Beethoven. It will have six seats from the concert hall and special VR headsets. You will be able to experience the VR production anywhere by a free app called Orchestra VR along with a virtual reality headset sold by Oculus and Samsung for $99.

I am not from the camp that says we must preserve traditional culture for its own sake. If something better or more relevant comes along, so be it. The new offerings, however, must have quality and depth.

What is disconcerting, however, is that people are shunting aside the highest quality literature, art and music produced by the greatest minds of the past. The classical arts presented the greatest triumphs and tragedies of history and the new generations need to inherit them for their lessons, inspiration and enjoyment. Today people seem to be abandoning the classical arts for violence, blasts of noise and color, and do-or-die drama reminiscent of the Roman coliseum games.

This can be a natural consequence of the boredom that smartphones have led us most to fear. In her book cited above, Sherry Turkle reports that people wind up being controlled by the technologies they embraced. They lose interest and skills in such basic human attributes as talk and discussion. She observes the demise of family conversations.

Children give up talking to their parents and vice versa. The family unit loses meaning other than economic. The mind cannot fully engage with the other conversant when both people are talking and texting simultaneously. Turkle observes that conversation is the most human and humanizing thing that we do and we are losing this skill. A consequence of this lack of conversation is that often values and shared history passed on through families from generation to generation and from teachers to students are diminished or lost.

We can hope that there will be highly engaging cultural productions that kids and everyone will easily find in the Knowosphere. Maybe in the future there will be a cycle where the family and village units as transmitters of culture will come to the fore again.

The Waiting Room Focus group

What do The People think? I recently had outpatient surgery and checked in at the clinic at 9:00 am, as did eight other patients. The staff called patients up to the check in desk and they returned when their paperwork was completed. Patients went through their pre-surgical prep, and were operated on and then discharged. This turned out to be essentially a focus group because after an hour or so of quietly waiting, the patients and their spouses started conversing with each other. These patients came from diverse walks of life.

I announced my book-in-progress about the rabbit hole to the group, and almost everyone perked up. The couple to my right looked like they might like to talk. He had been a state legislator for almost thirty years and was affable, but he was not very familiar with digital media. His wife, maybe ten years younger, jumped in, "I can't get along without this thing. Right now I'm arranging to pick up the kids."

"Do your kids have smartphones?" I asked her.

"Yes, and it keeps them from arts and music projects," she answered, anticipating my next question. "They just want to hang out with their friends." Other people in the group nodded and smiled knowingly.

"How can I manage a workable smartphone curfew?" she asked.

An older woman who sold candy and popcorn at a movie theater for many years, chimed in, "All this Internet and video stuff has ruined the movie business. The kids used to come in for wholesome movies and now they see everything at home or somewhere unless it is violent disgusting stuff which they can still see in the movie theater." This led to a lot of conversation about the film stars of the '30s and '40s.

Someone said, "Don't let the kids have smartphones until they're about twelve."

"Sounds like a substitute for Valium," someone else muttered.

A man who used to be a uranium miner said we should all take a breather and stay off digital half of the time. "You balance your yin and your yang," he said assertively, proud of his insight.

People started returning from the first round of surgery—I always seem to be last in waiting rooms—and despite their bandages, they wanted to talk. I evidently stirred them up. After everyone had some time to reflect on the issues, their common question boiled down to, "Will we all inevitably go down the rabbit hole?" They generally agreed that we were mostly there already. They also asked in various ways, a few looking at me searchingly, "If so, will we be able to get out?"

This conversation gives me hope. My waiting room survey indicates that people are aware and parents are concerned. The moguls of Silicon Valley may have seized the initial advantage in linking everybody and everything together digitally, but The People are beginning to recognize the consequences and should start pushing back.

11

RECAPTURING OUR MINDS

Some of the people in the waiting room recognized it: we must seize control of our minds again. The smartphone and the Internet should merely be tools and resources. They should help us to stimulate and improve our minds and to communicate easily with other minds but not control us. We need to seek mental balance for ourselves and certainly for our children.

To achieve mental balance, we must disconnect from the digital media from time to time. When we plug into the social media, online news, Google search, and video games, we are receiving information and raising our emotional levels through packaged entertainment. As long as this mental mode does not dominate us, that is okay.

Nevertheless, we must definitively disconnect from the digital media. We must flush the junk out of our minds and let our imaginations sparkle and our creativity flourish. How do we go about this?

Us versus the Computers

I have talked a lot in this book about almost all aspects of artificial intelligence technology. It makes much of our current economy, culture and lifestyle possible. It may even help in minimizing global warming. Nevertheless, I detect a great fear of the coming wave of super-smart computers and robots. People often tell me that they think computers will never be as smart as we are, but they are also afraid that computers will take over some day.

The essence of the matter is that humans do some things much better than computers, and these are things that require curiosity, imagination, sensitivity, and emotion. We can think of art, music, and deep sciences calling for these attributes.

Computers, on the other hand, can flawlessly process volumes of data far beyond any amount that we can imagine. The real threat to freedom and its attendant happiness may happen when a power-obsessed human combines with a gigantic super intelligent computer. Big Brother will have arrived.

This alliance overwhelms us so we do not know where the truth ends and fiction begins. Information sucked from the population rains down upon it. Answers that are apparently right because "everyone knows" substitute for science. In dealing with catastrophic phenomena like climate change, truth must trump belief.

As our world gets increasingly complex, it will be ever more tempting to turn the big thinking over to machines and artificial intelligence. We should always remind ourselves, however, that people, not machines, can have unfettered imagination and this produces bold new science, engineering, and art. This is paramount to our staying ahead of the machines.

Machines will continue to develop as evolutionary beings. They may become self-aware and self-improving. In time, they could develop emotion and conscience. They will coexist with humans along with all the other creatures and resources of the ecosphere. I believe however that the greatest threat to humankind is not computers gone mad, but humans who become demagogues by using ever smarter and dominant computers.

Time to Disconnect

Each of us probably has his or her own way of regaining control of our mind. For some it may be a long walk on the beach. For others it may be getting lost in a good book. For me it is taking a leisurely hike. I prefer a hilly area or a mountain where I can get a kaleidoscope of scenery and bracing fresh air.

As I start out, the trail curves through thick stands of leafy trees. It is early fall, and I wonder when the leaves will turn color this year. There are websites that have regional foliage forecasts, but it is more satisfying for me to observe all the signs of change. The squirrels and chipmunks are busily stashing seeds and nuts for the winter. They do not have smartphones to tell them anything. They just know.

As I work my way up the mountain, the leafy trees make way for spruce and pine evergreens. Flocks of chickadees and nuthatches are flitting from tree to tree picking away at the remnants of whatever tree or insect food they like. The trail becomes rocky. I awaken a somnolent snake on a flat rock outcropping absorbing the last warmth of the season before hibernating.

At last, I reach the summit and gaze out at the still valleys below. Nothing moves. There is only the rustle and tweets of creatures in the trees behind me and a hawk circling at summit level.

Nobody else is here today—the hiking season apparently is over—but there is a cluster of steel antennas a hundred yards away. I recall that they are relay antennas for telephone, government agencies, and cell phone services. I can power up my smartphone and plug in anywhere on earth. What are my Facebook friends saying? Does CNN have some vital breaking news? Has my credit card company extracted their monthly payment out of my bank account yet?

Suddenly none of the smartphone priorities seems important anymore. I can attend to them tomorrow if I am in the mood. Right now, I am going to search for a comfortable cushion of grass in a sheltered area and doze for a while. My brain is disengaged.

You should try different things to see what works for you.

- Take the family on a camping weekend in a nearby state park.
- Refresh yourself with a half-hour nap every day.
- Enroll in a course with weekly sessions. Yoga, watercolors, or a book club might distract you from the Web.

For something grander, and if you had the time and resources Audrey Hepburn had in the movie "*Sabrina*", you could escape to Paris for a cooking course. Overwhelmed by the developments at home, she said, "Be in and of the world and not just stand aside and watch."

How do you know when to disconnect from the Internet? The decision becomes more and more difficult as we come to depend on online activities. You used to pay the electric bill by check. Now the electric company withdraws their due automatically from your checking account. You used to welcome the crisp morning newspaper at breakfast and now you read pieces of it online during gaps in the day. By 10:00 a.m., you want to know where your children are—through smartphone tracking. You are looking into devices for seeing your dog's location by a smartphone map. And, of course, you must find out what everyone is saying on Facebook and see the pictures of their almost every moment on Instagram.

Are we becoming happier or more fulfilled? Are the social media helping us to find ourselves or are we sinking deeper into a state of anxiety, lack of self-esteem, and no empathy?

Although we know we should disconnect, or at least dial down, there seems to be no good time to disconnect. Perhaps you could create a dramatic moment of irrevocable decision. When I decided to quit smoking in my 20s, I was going up the stairway to the door of my plane (this was before jet ways from the terminal). Everyone was waiting for the engines to start and the plane to taxi. I looked out across the tarmac and the early morning rising mist. I threw my half-smoked pack of cigarettes out over the runway. It went end over end and landed by a perplexed ground crewperson. I never smoked again. Perhaps you could throw your smartphone off the bridge to the river far below in a similar fashion.

Disconnect for Children

"There is such a thing as everything" is what I overheard while passing a boy of about seven playing with some friends on a hiking trail. They were looking at flowers, trees, and butterflies and the entire ever-changing scene awed them. For a youngster who has not confronted the packaged information of the Knowosphere, this seemed like a perfectly reasonable thing to say.

These kids, however, may be a disappearing breed. A recent study by the Einstein Medical Center in Philadelphia, reported at the American Academy of Pediatrics meeting on April 25, 2015, states that "More than one-third of babies are tapping on smartphones and tablets even before they learn to walk or talk, and by 1 year of age, one in seven toddlers is using devices for at least an hour a day."[82] The parents who filled out the survey were at a hospital-based pediatric clinic that serves a low-income, minority community.

Thirty-six percent of the children tried using apps by the age of two, and the same percentage started playing video games at that age. Nearly two thirds of the parents used the digital media to calm their children and almost one-third of them used the digital media to get their children to sleep. Digital media are natural babysitters.

Dr. Hilda Kabali, leader of the study, said, "All the guidelines we have are based on TV, with the recommendation that viewing be limited to two hours a day, but most children aren't spending time on TV anymore. They're using tablets and smartphones."

Moving on to the child's consequent development, Dr. Kabali said, "Prolonged engagement in such activities limits parental interaction and can affect a child's capacity for social development, not to mention that too much sedentary entertainment can lead to obesity. Parents of children under the age of three should set significant limits and focus on reading and interacting. And once they're over three, they should also emphasize physical activity." For people living in the city, public parks are a good place to start the baby's exercise and to develop the baby's awareness of their surroundings.

Sherry Turkle in an interview with *National Public Radio* said, "Well, (if we have) no time to talk to our children... You're going to get children who don't know how to be a friend."[83]

What happens to these digitally raised kids? Victoria E. Dunkley, M.D., writing in *Psychology Today* says that electronic screen time makes kids angry, depressed and unmotivated. Dr. Dunkley has found that "Treating a child with mood dysregulation today requires methodically eliminating all electronics use for several weeks...to allow the nervous system to 'reset.'" She reports that "Time outdoors, especially interacting with nature, can restore attention, lower stress, and reduce aggression."[84]

Some Chinese scientists feel that the use of computer games among their children has taken an alarming turn. "Web Junky," a PBS video, reports that Chinese doctors consider this a clinical disorder and in some cases have confined children to rehabilitation centers sometimes for months.[85] The teenagers become addicted to video games and often do not eat, sleep or use the bathroom. One said, "Reality is too fake."

Jane E. Brodey in *The New York Times* reviewed the Chinese report along with other studies and concluded, "Technology is a poor substitute for personal interaction."[86] This corroborates Sherry Turkle's findings in her book, *Reclaiming Conversation: The Power of Talk in a Digital Age.*[87] Brodey went on to say that "Children who are heavy users of electronics may become adept at multitasking, but they can lose the ability to focus on what is most important, a trait critical to deep thought and problem solving needed for many jobs and other endeavors later in life."

As for my own anecdotal research, people I talk to who have children seem to gravitate to the point of view that their children should not have smartphones until their teens. If the younger children must have smartphones, their use needs to be limited to no more than one hour per day. I think this is a more restrictive attitude than a few years ago.

As troublesome as it may be, we must disconnect our children from the web most of the time.

The Importance of Imagination and Creativity

In our quest for a balanced mind, we must never forget that imagination and creativity are what gave us an edge over animals, climate changes and many other threats and obstacles. These attributes also are what ultimately will give us the advantage over computers, robots, and AI. Therefore, in recapturing our minds, we must stimulate our imagination and creativity to the max.

For the first time ever, humankind has received a fundamental way to improve everyone's creativity. We can use smartphones, the Knowosphere, AI and much more to overcome the dominance that those same digital media can have over us.

It is a question of maintaining control over our minds rather than letting the media control them.

Creativity is the driving force not only for producing great works of art or profound theories of physics. Creativity can produce a recipe for more flavorful and healthy muffins, or helping children express themselves using a variety of media. We should be trying to exercise our imagination and avoid just following other people's programming.

It is refreshing to see Albert Einstein's point of view on these matters:

> The important thing is not to stop questioning; curiosity has its own reason for existing. One cannot help but be in awe when contemplating the mysteries of eternity, of life, of the marvelous structure of reality. It is enough if one tries merely to comprehend a little of the mystery every day. The important thing is not to stop questioning; never lose a holy curiosity.[88]

The whole thing crystallized in my mind when I was in a remote village in Burma, now known as Myanmar. Through an interpreter, I asked a schoolteacher what she thought of robots (I never miss an opportunity to do book research!). She said, according to my notes, "The machines will take over a few things, then more things, until all you have to do is watch television. After many years, people will lose arms and legs for lack of use. You will turn into potatoes." That is the wisdom of a simple village woman. It is worth thinking about.

"Couch Potato" is of course, a common American expression, but now with virtual reality entertainment, the concept becomes more worrisome and real. If the technology reaches the point where the easiest thing to at any point is just to sit and watch, how far are we from potato land?

To avoid such a dystopia, people will have to do whatever is necessary to remain intellectually stimulated. They will have to exercise their curiosity and imagination just as they now work out in a gym to improve their physical health. As noted earlier in this chapter, if people connect or reconnect with nature they will find that it is their environment and ultimate support system. It is where we see analogs to human organizations and the human condition.

PREPARING THE NEW GENERATIONS

Years ago, I was on business in Mexico City, and after our sales discussions my Mexican friend invited my wife and I to his apartment for dinner with his family. After the usual pleasantries, the conversation turned to comparing differences in our countries. He said, "We think in many respects we have a better life here, but we are way behind you in pollution control. I had become concerned that you could hardly ever see the stars above at night. Then one night, while watching television, my daughter asked how big cows are. 'About as big as a large dog?' she asked." I was silent in disbelief. "So I took my family for a weekend in the country and we drove and drove until my daughter could see real cows. When we stayed overnight at her Aunt Maria's, she went out and kept pointing at the stars and wondered if they all have names." Thinking back, I still find this hard to believe, but in discussing it with my wife recently, she recalls the conversation in the same way.

While we cannot take our children all over the world to show them what everything looks like, it becomes more important than ever to impress upon them that the media at best only convey approximations to reality. We can use the digital media, however, to get closer to reality. When I was on that Mexico City trip, the Internet was hardly underway. Now my friend there could encourage his daughter to Google "vacas" (cows). Later, she could add to what she learned in the Knowosphere by a trip to a dairy.

Everyone, from children through grandparents, must learn how to use digital media as tools and not just as seemingly all-wise providers of information, social camaraderie, and entertainment. The key self-discipline children and adults must develop is to think for themselves before accepting everything they learn from the Internet and other media. When a new blast of "facts" arrives, the recipient's instinctive reaction should be to question the accuracy of the information using a concept rapidly becoming extinct, critical thinking.

As I have said in a number of ways in this book, we have reached a crossroads in the way people learn and think. Either we think first and follow-up on the Internet later, or we dive into the Internet, take what comes, and think about it if we have time. To avoid turning into a civilization enslaved by machine algorithms, I propose the following guidance for preparing the new generation.

1 – Make children feel important and listen to their questions and opinions

I recall that having my parents bat me down when I was attempting to offer an opinion among adults was one of my greatest developmental traumas. I felt unimportant and that I had nothing worth saying. Of course, parents often do not want their children breaking into a flow of conversation among adults, but a parent could say, "Come over and talk with us when we are all having coffee a little later."

If a child feels that adults, particularly parents, show a real interest in answering his questions or hearing what is on his mind, his ego boosts and he will not feel that he should always find or share information elsewhere. In the old days, kids would share dirty books and read them with a flashlight under the covers. Now they read the same thing on smart phones under the covers. The difference is that they can quickly decide that it is the parents' opinions that do not count. The Internet will be the place to go for everything.

The respect relationship must work both ways. We must remind children to respect their parents, teachers, and other people influential in their life. In some cases, the kids have a legitimate complaint. In discussions about daily problems in the digital age, children say that they do not talk to their parents anymore because the parents are constantly using their smartphones. Sherry Turkle and others suggest that children and parents should both stop Googling and talk.[89]

Everyone should have more empathy. We should develop conversation as a humanizing attribute. We could start at the dinner table.

2 – Children should learn to think for themselves and then learn about the Internet

Children should be encouraged to explore the world all around them in the traditional ways as soon as possible. This must be before they follow the cute little rabbit down the hole into mesmerizing Cyberland.

Children should always be able to explore, to find interesting books to read, to talk to interested adults, and most important, to find their own interest, passion, or vision at the earliest possible age. This is much more likely to happen if the children have retained their natural curiosity and imagination.

At this point, they can solve their problems, seek additional information, and begin to imagine whom they would like to be when they grow up. People start their skill set or career vision as early as four years old. It is never too early to start the mind on a lifelong productive course of action before the Internet captures it.

Only after the child has reached the point of considerable self-sufficiency in learning should the parents invest the time and funds to introduce the child to the Internet and all the digital devices to make it come alive. The parents should give the child digital devices, however, when the child can benefit from them. One organization with a helpful website is *Common Sense Media.*[90]

As soon as the child learns how to login to a tablet or smartphone, a parent or teacher should teach him or her how to use it productively. The child should learn how to use a search engine; how to see if a website is a genuine source of information or if it is an infomercial; and if an Internet information presentation is really programmed mainly to alter the mood and emotions of the viewer.

3 – The new world for students doing research

Everyone should know that we are in a paradigm shift with respect to knowledge acquisition and understand that there are serious consequences for sloppy data interpretation. We must be sure that children understand the differences between "good information" and "bad information" starting in the first year in school.

I woke up to this emerging reality recently when judging an elementary school science fair. This school was serving the poorest part of town with many of the students being the children of undocumented Mexican immigrants. They were bright eyed and anxious to show their exhibits of such things as the way plants grow with different nutrients and demonstrations of gravity and motion.

As I talked to the kids, it dawned on me that they were getting a lot of their project ideas and help from the Internet. Some kids were getting their project designs from Web-based services catering to science fair students. I estimated that 20% of those in grade two and 80% in grade six were doing this. There is a warning sign here that the unconditional use of Internet packages may have proliferated due to an emphasis on right answers and attractive demonstrations with a disregard of the science involved. On the positive side, maybe the Internet set the kids' minds in motion, and perhaps they will embark on fruitful scientific careers.

About that time, I saw an article by Monica Hesse in the *Washington Post* where she asked, "For the Google Generation, what happens to the concepts of truth and knowledge in a user-generated world of information saturation?"[91] She reports on a college freshman who never checked out a book from the university library, but all of the Internet information overwhelmed her. The student remarked, "The idea of having an original thought terrified me." Once she realized how much information was out there, the idea of productively using it seemed impossible. Knowing how to filter out irrelevant information is part of learning.

We must inculcate the value and methods of good research in our student population. As they enter the enterprise world, be it public or private, profit or non-profit, they must have and maintain a critical attitude towards information, knowledge, truth, creative ideas, invention, flights of fancy and imagination. Then they will realize that the pursuit of new scientific insights must include focusing on finding truth among all the information and not just processing the information itself. Without the sense of importance of empirical truth, people forget the relevance of reality.

We will need many graduates excited by the challenge of the unknown. The wonders revealed to them in their explorations will captivate them. The goal of making unique contributions to solving the world's problems will sustain them.

4 – Technical and career education

Discussions today about restoring the economic health of the country and bettering the job prospects for new entrants into the work force often lead to calls for more creativity and entrepreneurship. I have a lot of first-hand experience in this process because I spent much of my life as a creative engineer and business owner. If I were to start again today, I would take full advantage of the tools of the digital media and the Internet. In my two startup high tech companies, we used software in product designs and business management more than our competitors did.

I know from my own career success that formal education is very important for entrepreneurs. I have a master's degree. As has always been the case, however, many of those with creative minds tend to be impatient and often drop out of school before they complete their education. They become frustrated with the formality and rigid structure they perceive to be endemic to classroom education. There is a tension between the accumulation of facts and nurturing creativity. There does not seem to be any room left for the mind to wander, catch a glimpse of a new vision, or pursue it wherever it may lead.

In the twenty-first century, the quantity of information is growing so rapidly that it is impossible to select what to teach to students as the basis of The Knowledge that they will need in the future. Besides teaching the basics, schools will have to focus on providing students with the skills they need to be able to solve problems and answer questions that have not yet arisen

There is agreement that American students are weak in the STEM (science, technology, engineering, and mathematics) courses compared to students in most other advanced countries.[92] STEM education must include computer technology and coding because these skills are called for in all fields of endeavor. People who do not learn at least some coding and computer applications are in danger of being among the first that robots and artificial intelligence will replace.

Continuing education for adults is more important than ever because technology and its applications are changing so rapidly. An adult can change job specialties or careers three or more times in a lifetime. Fortunately, career-based education is easily accessible with community colleges, online courses and other easy-to-use offerings.

Correspondence schools and community colleges traditionally have been a source of second start education for those who grew to realize that they did not learn enough to achieve some aspiration. Some universities including MIT are offering their courses free online to anyone who logs in to them. Called Massive Open Online Course or MOOCs they are a definite second chance for some self-directed individuals.

Where possible in such cases however, it would be very helpful to have a coach or tutor critique and guide the otherwise self-guided student as they try to sort out this stream of knowledge. With highly interactive computer clouds offering multimedia education in a reality-based dialogue method, the students could find themselves in a virtual classroom with personal attention.

When students become employees in industry or government, they often will find more interest in new ideas than seemed to be the case in schools, especially if employed in technical areas such as engineering. However, deficiency of essential formal education often shows up in these career choices as lack of essential technical knowledge or communication skills.

I have encountered many entrepreneurial technicians and engineers who hit a brick wall because they did not know the physics or chemistry involved in their inventions. It is very difficult to catch up in deep technical areas later in life. They would have benefited by studying more science and math while in schools and universities. The areas of significant technical invention today usually are much more complex than in Thomas Edison's day, so prospects are much dimmer for the essentially self-taught entrepreneurs.

Equally, an obstacle is the lack of communication abilities on the part of these entrepreneurial hopefuls. They cannot seem to explain in understandable language what they are thinking or proposing. They cannot read published information that is required to support their project. They cannot write down their findings and notes for their associates and followers.

5 – Long term attributes for success

Parents, counselors, teachers, and others guiding the younger generation should try everything to increase the youngsters' curiosity, imagination, and vision. They must help these new adults find a passion, which will carry them through the hard times, like cooking or gardening. Perhaps offer the idea of a mission like the military or supplying medical and spiritual help for the homeless. Or, perhaps even starting the next Google.

All along their life path, these young people will be well served by having self-confidence. If you do not believe in yourself, most other people will not believe in you either. My self-confidence was about all that rescued me during several unexpected job losses.

Successful people in any profession learn from both their advances and their difficulties. They never give up. They focus on their vision and on the truth as clearly as they can see it. Despite what anyone says, successful people do not give up.

Times of insight and creativity come and go with the ebb and flow of unexploited knowledge and with society's sense of urgency for new solutions. The industrial revolution and World War II were eras that saw surges of insights, creativity and invention. Now the world is benefiting from a combination of bright new minds coming up through the educational systems, well-equipped laboratories and shops, and the new information sources of the computer clouds; but there is an apocalyptic sense of the world running out of time. Many people feel a sense of "Why bother?" because it appears that the world has run out of possibilities.

People must see that virtually all knowledge and data is available to them and that creativity has never been more important than now. Children can be excited to expect that there is an infinite future for them. Society's failure is the failure to give them hope and encouragement. Children are the future.

Now is the time for the men and women who dream of things that never were. Their dreams and visions are the starting points in great creations and in solving problems previously thought unsolvable; and their positive emotions will energize everyone. Not even the sky is the limit.

13

THE ROAD AHEAD

Computers do not seek meaning in life. They do not have consciousness. Yet in the digital world, computers are changing the lives of receptive humans. I do not know whether this is good or bad, but if the present trends continue, what it means to be human will change.

As long as we humans are the dominant species, the human brain will be more important than computers. We know how computers work, but understanding the brain's inner workings is still a slow work in progress. In view of all the recurring news about advancements in the digital media, it may be helpful to step back and see how impressive the human brain is.

The component of the brain called the neocortex is what makes us most human. It is the outer layer of the upper hemisphere of the brain and consists of six layers. Its functions include sensory perception, the ability to learn with behavioral flexibility, motor commands, conscious thought, and, in humans, language. In humans, the neocortex is 90% of the cerebral cortex compared to a very minor percentage evidenced in simple mammals.

Another important part of the brain, which makes it a superb thinking machine, is the prefrontal cortex behind the forehead. It relates current perceptions to memories of experiences in order to provide an executive and planning function for judging priorities and future planning. It plays a critical role in the regulation of emotion, and it is the storage area for short-term memory. The prefrontal cortex is involved with decision-making, problem-solving, and integration of ideas. Other mammals, particularly primates such as monkeys, have prefrontal cortices but not as developed as those in human brains.

The fundamental component of information storage in the neocortex is the neuron, a biological cell. The neurons have information gates called synapses to connect by electrochemical signaling to other neurons. The neocortex nodes are the intersection of billions of interconnected synapses resulting in a virtually solid mass of ultrafine wiring. Spread around in there are all your memories, skills, and the pathways interconnecting them. According to David Eagleman's book *The Brain*, the neocortex has about one quadrillion (1×10^{15}) synapses. This is about a billion synapses per cubic millimeter—an unimaginably compact packing density.[93]

The number of synapses is the most important number because it is a rough approximation of the brain's information recognition capacity. The bottom line is that the human brain has enough memory capacity to accommodate most reasoning and cognitive tasks and a lifetime of memories.

The map or wiring diagram of all the quadrillion interconnections in your brain is unique to you and is a collection of all of your life experiences and memories. The name of this map is the "connectome." Someday, perhaps decades from now, we should be able to transfer a complete copy of the brain into a mega computer. While theoretically possible, the technical and engineering challenges are immense.

A very active computer sciences application area is using artificial intelligence programming to make a computer system work like a brain. As discussed in Chapter 5, the public really became aware of big AI when IBM's ultra super AI computer, Watson, beat two former winners of the television quiz show *Jeopardy!*[94] It uses IBM's *DeepQA* technology to generate hypotheses, gather massive evidence, and continue analyzing the data until it can propose a solution. Creativity, however, was not part of the design for this AI computer, assuming that was even possible.

IBM's current research is to design systems that can learn from and interact with people. As Guruduth S. Banavar, director of IBM's cognitive computing research, told the *New York Times*, "The result should be way better than either a human or a computer system can do alone."[95]

IBM has a goal of supplying devices for a 100 trillion synapse supercomputer—about the synapse count in the human brain—and at that point we will be well on our way to making HAL in *2001: A Space Odyssey* or the female computer person in the movie *Her.* Its energy consumption would be considerably less than a digital computer of similar capability, but much more than the human brain (about 20 watts). The power consumption issue will be an area for further improvement of the technology.

Exciting as many of your synapses as possible is the challenge for the search services, social media, and digital media companies. These include Google, Facebook, and Sony. All of them are experimenting with artificial intelligence and virtual reality to communicate with you smoothly and pleasingly. An unstated goal will be to maintain your "connection" with the computer system as long as possible. Welcome user benefits will include extremely accurate searches and other services tailored to you, and communications between people and computers totally by voice. This is digital rabbit hole 2.0.

I believe however, that we should not give in to electronic brains. This means keeping our conscious and subconscious mind mostly free from digital influence. We must always remember that how each human being responds to the world around them depends on a composite of all the information in his or her conscious and subconscious mind. Your genes, your family and neighborhood, your environment and travel experiences, your education, accumulated perceptions and more program your brain.

Endowing machines with emotion,—which seems impossible but almost certainly is not—will be the tipping point where people will really have to fight back against machines. Think how emotion has magnified the impact of speech, literature, movies, Internet messages and more. Research is going on in many AI and robot labs to have machines detect and characterize human emotion and to respond to it with simulated emotion.

In the conclusion of *The Brain* Eagleman wrote:

> Only one thing is certain: our species is just at the beginning of something, and we don't fully know what it is. We're at an unprecedented moment in history, one in which brain science and technology are co-evolving. What happens at this intersection is poised to change who we are...We're capable of inhabiting new sensory realities and new kinds of bodies. Eventually, we may be able to shed our physical forms altogether.[96]

How do we make sure humanity maintains control of all the human brains and yet benefits from digital devices and the limitless Internet to the greatest extent possible? My friend Jim Rutt, Internet pioneer and past CEO of Network Solutions, wrote to me "How we deal with the coming 'real AI' wave will be a major inflection point in human history. How long it stays just 'human' history is another story!"

With the smartphone, the Internet and other digital media, we have wonderful tools, but we must be careful in their use. Both family and school education must include lessons from experience about where and how to use digital media. It will be included along with such staples as sports and sex education. If we can make the smart phone, the Internet of things, and AI into tools useful to humans, not just to institutions, and not replacements for ourselves, we can succeed as a species.

Humans have to figure out how to make computers work for everyone's benefit. Mechanics, farmers, artists, musicians, inventors, teachers, politicians and all occupations and professions must benefit. This must be without compromise to people's freedoms, and their ability to determine the truth.

I do not have any technology solutions. Technology will press ahead no matter what fixes are imbedded in it.

To rise above this digital technology onslaught, we must be positive. We will develop a renewed sense of purpose. We will not allow ourselves to fall down a digital rabbit hole and we will protect others from doing the same. We will be creative and not become passive consumers in a personalized niche in the Cyberweb. We will allow the Internet to be part of our presence but not all the time. We should obligate ourselves to regularly disconnect from the digital world and reconnect with each other, our communities, the environment and ourselves.

We must also maintain mental independence. This means thinking for ourselves, and vigilantly verifying the truthfulness of information. We have to remind ourselves that genuine knowledge is more important and valuable than information masquerading as knowledge and insight. This experience will lead us on to wisdom.

We are living in an era of profound transformations. This is the time when there are unprecedented technology and environmental changes. Meanwhile, we are trying to reconcile human intelligence with machine intelligence. The human species may be achieving well below its possibilities. Let's recapture our destiny!

We need to develop new ideas and knowledge. This begins with the creative process leading to new art, science, innovation, environmental and economic development. We will have to emerge from our digital rabbit holes having enjoyed the adventure, but eager to move on to greater things.

That's all folks!

ACKNOWLEDGEMENTS

First, special thanks go to Joe Stetter, Bob Eisenstein, John Schultz and Grant Holland who read the book and made helpful comments. They are scientists and engineers and focused on the technical issues. I would also like to thank Virginia Wagner Ross, Deborah Morningstar, Robert Christie, and Diane Smiroldo who were readers and offered great insights. My editors were the dynamic team of Cynde Christie and Sarah Lovett who worked tirelessly on all aspects of the manuscript and cheered me on. I greatly benefitted from the discussions I have had with friends at the Santa Fe Institute including Jeremy Sabloff, Geoffrey West, and David Krakouer. Through it all, my wife Betsy has been my rock solid advisor and cheerleader.

ABOUT THE AUTHOR

Larry Kilham is a Sloan School of Management graduate from MIT. He has received three patents and has founded two high-tech companies. Many of his product designs required innovative use of computers, and as early as the 1960s he was researching artificial intelligence (AI).

After selling his last business, Larry has written three novels with AI themes and two books about creativity, invention, and high tech management. He has long wanted to write this book about digital media, describing its opportunities for advancement and its impacts on humanity.

Larry and his wife Betsy live in Santa Fe, New Mexico. More information about his books and his blog can be found at www.LarryKilham.net. He can be contacted at lkilham@gmail.com.

CREDITS

Cover – Rabbit
  IR Stone/Shutterstock.com.
Introduction – Rabbit
  Public domain
Chapter 1 - Chart – Literacy
  L. Kilham
Chapter 2 - Selfie queen
  © 2015 Alice Griffin
Chapter 2 – Friend request from castle
  Cartoonresource/Shutterstock.com
Chapter 3 – DIKW pyramid
  Public domain
Chapter 6 – Girl wearing VR googles
  Aleksandra Suzi/Shutterstock.com
Chapter 6 - Samurai sword fight
  Igor Zakowski/Shutterstock.com
Chapter 8 – Venn Diagram
  L. Kilham
Chapter 11 – Young girl working on iPad
  CroMary/Shutterstock.com
Chapter 13 – Rabbit peering out of hole
  Red_in_Woman/Shutterstock.com

REFERENCES

Introduction

[1] Carroll, Lewis with original illustrations by John Tenniel, (2015). *Alice's Adventures in Wonderland and Through the Looking Glass: 150ᵗʰ Anniversary Edition,* New York, Penguin Classics Deluxe.

Chapter 1 The Rise of the Smartphones

[2] Greenfield, Susan, (2005, February). From "We are the Final Frontier," by Ian Sample, *The Guardian.* guardian.co.uk. http://www.theguardian.com/education/2005/feb/10/ science.highereducation.

[3] Bilton, Nick, (2014, September). "Steve Jobs was a Low Tech Parent," *New York Times.* http://www.nytimes.com/2014/09/11/ fashion/steve-jobs-apple-was-a-low-tech-parent.html.

[4] Pew research Center, Internet, Science & Technology, *U.S. Smartphone Use in 2015,* http://www.pewinternet. org/2015/04/01/us-smartphone-use-in-2015.

[5] ComScore Reports, (2015, September). "U.S. Smartphone Subscriber Market Share." http://www.prnewswire.com/news-releases/comscore-reports-september-2015-us-smartphone-subscriber-market-share-300174058.html.

[6] Warzel, Charlie, (2013, October). "Here's the Cold, Hard Proof that We Can't Stop Checking our Smartphones," *BuzzFeed News.* http://www.buzzfeed.com/charliewarzel/heres-the-cold-hard-proof-that-we-cant-stop-checking-our-pho#.pmR7O7d7k.

[7] Brody, Jane E., (2015, July) "Screen Addiction Is Taking a Toll on Children," *New York Times.* http://well.blogs.nytimes.com/2015/07/06/screen-addiction-is-taking-a-toll-on-children.

[8] Meeker, Mary, "2015 Internet Trends Report" (Slide presentation). http://www.slideshare.net/kleinerperkins/internet-trends-v1.

[9] Miller, Claire Cain and Birmingham, Chi, (2014, May). "A Vision of the Future," *New York Times.* http://www.nytimes.com/interactive/2014/05/02/upshot/FUTURE.

[10] Darlin, Damon, (2014, November). "Cashless Society? It's Already Coming," *New York Times.* http://www.nytimes.com/2014/11/29/upshot/cashless-society-its-already-coming.html?_r=0.

[11] Wikipedia, "Internet of Things," https://en.wikipedia.org/wiki/Internet_of_Things.

[12] "Leading online video games worldwide in 2013," Statista.com, http://www.statista.com/statistics/328683/leading-online-video-games.

[13] Bauerlein, Mark, (2008). *The Dumbest Generation: How the Digital Age Stupefies Young Americans and Jeopardizes Our Future,* Jeremy P. Tarcher/ New York, Penguin, P. xii.

[14] Educational Testing Service (ETS) PIAAC report on skills of Millennials. "AMERICA'S SKILLS CHALLENGE: Millennials and the Future," The ETS Center for Research on Human Capital and Education. http://www.ets.org/s/research/30079/asc-millennials-and-the-future.pdf.

[15] For more on selfies see:
Day, Elizabeth, (2013, July). "How selfies became a global phenomenon," *The Guardian.* http://www.theguardian.com/technology/2013/jul/14/how-selfies-became-a-global-phenomenon.

Fox, Jesse and Rooney Margaret C., (2015, April). "The Dark Triad and trait self-objectification as predictors of men's use and self-presentation behaviors on social networking sites, *Personality and Individual Differences.* http://www.sciencedirect.com/science/article/pii/S0191886914007259.

Murphy, Kate, (2015, August). "What Selfie Sticks Really Tell Us About Ourselves," *The New York Times.* http://www.nytimes.com/2015/08/09/sunday-review/what-selfie-sticks-really-tell-us-about-ourselves.

Sanghani, Radhika, (2015, August). "Why we really take selfies: the 'terrifying' reasons explained," *The Telegraph.* http://www.telegraph.co.uk/women/10760753/Why-we-really-take-selfies-the-terrifying-reasons-explained.html.

Chapter 2 Digital Media Addiction

[16] Mazlish, Bruce, (1993, October). "A Highway or a Trap?" *New York Times* book review.

[17] Smith, David, (2015, January). "Google Chairman: 'The Internet Will Disappear," *Business Insider.* http://www.businessinsider.com/google-chief-eric-schmidt-the-internet-will-disappear-2015-1.

[18] Barr, N. et al, (2015, July). "The brain in your pocket: Evidence that Smartphones are used to supplant thinking," *Computers in Human Behavior.* http://www.sciencedirect.com/science/article/pii/S0747563215001272.

[19] Clark, A., (2008). *Supersizing the mind: Embodiment, action, and cognitive extension,* England, Oxford University Press.

Clark, A., and Chalmers, D., (2019, July). "The Extended Mind," *Analysis.* http://postcog.ucd.ie/files/TheExtendedMind.pdf.

[20] Aoki, Kumiko and Downes, Edward J., (2003, February). "An analysis of young people's use of and attitudes toward cell phones," *Telematics and Informatics.* http://www.angelfire.com/ego2/lostboyrahul/work/cellphoneuse.pdf.

[21] Clayton, Russell B., Leshner, Glenn, and Almon, Anthony, (2015, January). "The Extended iSelf: The Impact of iPhone Separation on Cognition, Emotion, and Physiology," *Journal of Computer-Mediated Communication.* http://onlinelibrary.wiley.com/doi/10.1111/jcc4.12109/full.

22 *World Travel Market Global Trends Report 2013.* Click on "News" tab and then enter "Detox" in search bar. http://www.hospitalitynet.org/news/4062821.html.

23 Turkle, Sherry, (2011). *Alone Together: Why We Expect More from Technology and Less from Each Other,* New York, Basic Books.

24 Smith, Aaron, (2011, September). "Americans and Text Messaging," *Pew Research Center.* http://www.pewinternet.org/2011/09/19/americans-and-text-messaging.

25 Willingham, Daniel T., (2015, January). "Smartphones Don't Make Us Dumb," *New York Times.* http://www.nytimes.com/2015/01/21/opinion/smartphones-dont-make-us-dumb.html.

26 Common Sense Media, (2015, November). "Media Use by Tweens and Teens." https://www.commonsensemedia.org/research/the-common-sense-census-media-use-by-tweens-and-teens.

Chapter 3 The Knowosphere:
The Infinite World of No Escape

27 Teilhard de Chardin, Pierre, (2008). *The Phenomenon of Man,* New York, Harper Perennial Modern Classics.

28 Moreau de Maupertuis, Pierre Louis, Wikipedia.org. https://en.wikipedia.org/wiki/Pierre_Louis_Maupertuis.

[29] Houghton, Samuel, (1872, April). "The Principle of Least Action in Nature," Three lectures given at Trinity College, Dublin, Ireland, summarized in Pacific Rural Press, Volume 3, Number 17. http://cdnc.ucr.edu/cgi-bin/cdnc?a=d&d=PRP18720427.2.12.3.

[30] Google's Tally of World Book Titles: 129,864,880, (2010). *National Public Radio.* http://www.npr.org/templates/story/story.php?storyId=129160859.

[31] Wikipedia: Size of Wikipeda. https://en.wikipedia.org/wiki/Wikipedia:Size_of_Wikipedia.

[32] The GovLab Index: The Data Universe, (2013, August). http://thegovlab.org/govlab-index-the-digital-universe.

[33]."Big Data, for better or worse: 90% of world's data generated over last two years," (2013, May). Science Daily. www.sciencedaily.com/releases/2013/05/130522085217.htm .

[34] "A Comprehensive List of Big Data Statistics," Wikibon Blog. http://wikibon.org/blog/big-data-statistics.

[35] "World-wide Internet Usage Facts and Statistics—2013," factshunt.com. http://www.factshunt.com/2014/01/world-wide-internet-usage-facts-and.html.

[36] IDC: "The Digital Universe in 2020: Big Data, Bigger Digital Shadows, and Biggest Growth in the Far East." http://www.emc.com/leadership/digital-universe/2012iview/index.htm.

[37] Diamandis, Peter, (2015, May). "The World in 2025: 8 Predictions for the Next 10 Years," *SingularityHub* published by Singularity

University. http://singularityhub.com/2015/05/11/the-world-in-2025-8-predictions-for-the-next-10-years.

Chapter 4 The Best Uses of the Knowosphere

[38] For a comprehensive description of the library of Alexandria, see Wikipedia, Library of Alexandria. https://en.wikipedia.org/wiki/Library_of_Alexandria.

[39] "History Of Servers in Pictures, from 1981 to today." *iWeb Hosting Blog.* http://blog.iweb.com/en/2012/01/history-of-servers-in-pictures-from-1981-to-today/1959.html.

[40] "A Comprehensive List of Big Data Statistics," Wikibon Blog. http://wikibon.org/blog/big-data-statistics.

[41] Kilham, Larry, (2015). *MegaMinds: Creativity and Invention,* FutureBooks.info. http://www.amazon.com/MegaMinds-Creativity-Invention-Larry-Kilham/dp/1505920957.

[42] Private communication.

Chapter 5 The Shadow of AI and Robots

[43] For more on the Google Deep Mind and Neural Networks projects, see:

"Inceptionism: Going Deeper into Neural Networks," Google Research Blog. http://googleresearch.blogspot.com/2015/06/inceptionism-going-deeper-into-neural.html.

"A Neural Conversational Model," Vinyals, Oriol and Le, Quoc V., Google, arvix.org. http://arxiv.org/pdf/1506.05869.pdf.

Levy Steven, "The Deep Mind of Demis Hassabis," *medium. com.* https://medium.com/backchannel/the-deep-mind-of-demis-hassabis-156112890d8a.

[44] Barrie, Joseph, (2014, November). "Computers Are Writing Novels: Read A Few Samples Here," *BusinessInsider.com.* http://www.businessinsider.com/novels-written-by-computers-2014-11.

[45] Markoff, John, (2013, December). "Brainlike Computers, Learning from Experience," *The New York Times.* http://www.nytimes.com/2013/12/29/science/brainlike-computers-learning-from-experience.html?pagewanted=all&_r=0.

[46] Markoff, John, "IBM Develops a New Chip That Functions Like a Brain," (2014, August). *The New York Times.* http://www.nytimes.com/2014/08/08/science/new-computer-chip-is-designed-to-work-like-the-brain.html.

[47]. Frey, Carl Benedikt and Osborne, Michael, A., (2013, September). "The Future of Employment: How Susceptible are Jobs to Computerisation?" UK, Oxford University. http://www.futuretech.ox.ac.uk/sites/futuretech.ox.ac.uk/files/The_Future_of_Employment_OMS_Working_Paper_0.pdf.

[48] Von Drehle, David, (2013, September). "The Robot Economy," *Time.* http://content.time.com/time/magazine/article/0,9171,2150607,00.html.

[49] Brynjolfsson, Erik and McAfee, Andrew, (2011). *Race Against the Machine*, Digital Frontier Press.

[50] This theme is discussed in detail in Kilham, Larry, (2014). *Winter of the Genomes*, FutureBooks. Info. http://www.amazon.com/Winter-Genomes-Larry-Kilham/dp/1500822051.

[51] Turkle, Sherry, (2011). *Alone Together: Why We Expect More from Technology and Less from Each Other*, New York, Basic Books.

Chapter 6 Virtual Reality and Me

[52] For an illustrated overview of the emerging world of VR, see Stein, Joel, (2015, April). "The Surprising Joy of Virtual Reality and Why it's about to Change the World," *Time*. pp. 40-49. http://time.com/3987022/why-virtual-reality-is-about-to-change-the-world.

[53] Ars Electronica Center, Linz, Austria, http://www.aec.at/center/en/.

[54] Virtual Reality Studies: GreenlightVR. http://www.greenlightvr.com.

[55] Virtual Reality Google Cardboard viewer: http://www.google.com/get/cardboard.

[56] See, for example, Parkinson, Hannah Jane, (2015, September). "Seven Wonders of the World to Explore on Google Street View," *The Guardian*.

http://www.theguardian.com/technology/2015/sep/18/
seven-wonders-of-the-world-google-street-view?CMP=ema_565.

Chapter 7 Decisions

[57] Krakauer, David, interview with Steve Paulson, (2015, April). "Ingenious: David Krakauer" in *Nautilus* magazine. http://nautil.us/issue/23/dominoes/ingenious-david-krakauer.

[58] Huxley, Aldous, (2013). *Brave New World*, Everyman's Library, New York.

[59] Kilham, Larry, (2014). *Winter of the Genomes*, FutureBooks. Info, pp. 55-56. http://www.amazon.com/Winter-Genomes-Larry-Kilham/dp/1500822051.

[60] See, for example, Sifferlin, Alexandra, (2015, November). "Why (almost) everyone is embracing the digital doctor," *Time*. http://time.com/4092350/why-almost-everyone-is-embracing-the-digital-doctor.

Chapter 8 Decisions

[61] Fisher, Matthew, Goddu, Mariel K., and Keil, Frank C., (2015, March). "Search for Explanations: How the Internet Inflates Estimates of Internal Knowledge," *Journal of Experimental Psychology: General*. http://www.apa.org/pubs/journals/releases/xge-0000070.pdf.

[62] Kilham, Larry, (2015). *MegaMinds: Creativity and Invention,* Chapters 8-11. FutureBooks.info. http://www.amazon.com/ MegaMinds-Creativity-Invention-Larry-Kilham/dp/1505920957.

[63] Barrow, John, (2005, February). "Humans Become a Collective Intelligence," in "We are the final frontier," *The Guardian.* http://www.theguardian.com/education/2005/feb/10/ science.highereducation.

Barrow, John, (2006). *The Infinite Book, New York,* Vintage.

[64] MIT Center for Collective Intelligence, http://cci.mit.edu/. A good overview and library of working papers about collective intelligence.

Kilham, Larry, (2015, April). "Collective Intelligence for Mega Problem Solving," *Huffington Post* guest blog. http://www.huffingtonpost.com/larry-kilham/collective-intel-ligence-f_b_7056494.html?1428949101.

[65] Malone, Thomas W., (2014). "How the MIT Climate CoLab Harnesses Collective Intelligence to Combat Climate Change," *MIT Sloan Management Review,* pp. 22-25.

[66]. Malone, Thomas W. et al, (2009, February). "Harnessing Crowds: Mapping the Genome of Collective Intelligence," Working Paper No. 2009-001, MIT Center for Collective Intelligence. http://cci.mit.edu/publications/CCIwp2009-01.pdf.

[67] InnoCentive see http://www.innocentive.com.

[68] Zweig, Mark and DeVoto, Emily, "Observational Studies—Does The Language Fit The Evidence?—Association Versus Causation," *Health News Review,* undated. http://www.health-newsreview.org/toolkit/tips-for-understanding-studies/does-the-language-fit-the-evidence-association-versus-causation.

Chapter 9 Advancement, Education, and Creativity

[69] Postman, Neil, (2005). *Amusing Ourselves to Death: Public Discourse in the Age of Show Business.* New York, Penguin.

[70] Huxley, Aldous, (2013). *Brave New World,* New York, Everyman's Library.

[71] Weisenbaum, Joseph, (1984). *Computer Power and Human Reason,* New York, Penguin Books.

[72] Chaitin, Gregory, (2012). *Proving Darwin: Making Biology Mathematical,* New York, Pantheon.

Chapter 10 The Internet and the People

[73] Sagan, Carl, (2003). *The Demon-Haunted World: Science as a Candle in the Dark,* New York, Random House.

[74] Turkle, Sherry, (2015). *Reclaiming Conversation: The Power of Talk in a Digital Age,* New York, Penguin.

[75] Anderson, Monica and Perrin Andrew, (2015, July). "15% of Americans don't use the internet. Who are they?" *Pew Research Center.* http://www.pewresearch.org/fact-tank/2015/07/28/15-of-americans-dont-use-the-internet-who-are-they.

[76] Smith, David, (2015, January). "Google Chairman: 'The Internet Will Disappear," *Business Insider.* http://www.businessinsider.com/google-chief-eric-schmidt-the-internet-will-disappear-2015-1.

[77] Franzen, Jonathan, review of Turkle, Sherry, (2015, October). *Reclaiming Conversation: The Power of Talk in a Digital Age, New York Times Book Review.* http://www.nytimes.com/2015/10/04/books/review/jonathan-franzen-reviews-sherry-turkle-reclaiming-conversation.html.

[78] Vanhoenacker, Mark, (2014, January). "Requiem. Classical Music in America is Dead," *Slate.com.* http://www.slate.com/articles/arts/culturebox/2014/01/classical_music_sales_decline_is_classical_on_death_s_door.html.

[79] Birkerts, Sven, (2015). *Changing the Subject: Art and Attention in the Internet Age, New York,* Graywolf Press.

[80] Hobsbawm, Eric, (2014). *Fractured Times: Culture and Society in the Twentieth Century,* New York, The New Press.

[81] Hempel, Jessi, (2015, September). "LA's Philharmonic is Bringing the Symphony to Everyone—in VR," *Wired.* http://www.wired.com/2015/09/la-philharmonic-vr.

Chapter 11 Recapturing Our Minds

[82] Einstein Medical Center Study by Dr. Hilda Kabali about infants using mobile media:

Einstein Medical Center, (2015, April). "Toddler Tweets? Maybe Not so Far Off," Press release. http://www.einstein.edu/news/toddler-tweets-maybe-not-so-far-off.

American Academy of Pediatrics, (2015, April). "Babies as young as 6 months using mobile media," Press release. http://www.eurekalert.org/pub_releases/2015-04/aaop-bay041715.php.

Kaplan, Karen, (2015, April). "More Than a Third of Infants Are Using Smartphones, Tablets, Study Says," *Los Angeles Times.* http://www.latimes.com/science/sciencenow/la-sci-sn-babies-screen-time-iphone-ipad-20150424-story.html.

[83] Turkle, Sherry, (2015, September). "Making the Case For Face To Face In an Era of Digital Conversation," Interview with *National Public Radio (NPR).* http://www.npr.org/2015/09/26/443480452/making-the-case-for-face-to-face-in-an-era-of-digital-conversation.

[84] Dunckley, Victoria L., (2015, August). "Screentime Is Making Kids Moody, Crazy and Lazy," *Psychology Today.* https://www.psychologytoday.com/blog/mental-wealth/201508/screentime-is-making-kids-moody-crazy-and-lazy.

[85] Obsessive gaming among Chinese teenagers: "Web Junkie," PBS Video. http://video.pbs.org/video/2365526899.

86 Brody, Jane E., (2015, July). "Screen Addiction is Taking a Toll on Children," *New York Times.* http://well.blogs.nytimes.com/2015/07/06/screen-addiction-is-taking-a-toll-on-children.

87 Turkle, Sherry, (2015). *Reclaiming Conversation: The Power of Talk in a Digital Age,* New York, Penguin.

88 Einstein, Albert, (1955, May). From statement to William Miller, as quoted in *Life* magazine.

Chapter 12 Preparing the New Generations

89 Turkle Sherry, (2015, September). "Stop Googling. Let's Talk." *The New York Times.* http://www.nytimes.com/2015/09/27/opinion/sunday/stop-googling-lets-talk.html.

90 Common Sense Media. https://www.commonsensemedia.org.

91 Hesse, Monica, (2008, April). "Truth: Can You Handle it? Better Yet: Do You know It When You See It," *The Washington Post.* http://www.washingtonpost.com/wp-dyn/content/article/2008/04/25/AR2008042500922.html.

92 STEM – U.S. Department of Education. http://www.ed.gov/stem.

Chapter 13 The Road Ahead

93 Eagleman, David, (2015). *The Brain,* New York, Pantheon Books, and the PBS TV series by the same name.

[94] "Watson (computer)," http://en.wikipedia.org/wiki/Watson_(computer).

[95] Lohr, Steve, (2014, June). "Intelligence too Big for a Machine," *The New York Times.* http://bits.blogs.nytimes.com/2014/06/11/intelligence-too-big-for-a-single-machine.

[96] Eagleman, *op. cit.*, p. 201.

www.ingramcontent.com/pod-product-compliance
Lightning Source LLC
Chambersburg PA
CBHW031239050326
40690CB00007B/878